101 MORE WAYS TO ENJOY RETIREMENT

ENGAGING ACTIVITIES, CRAFTS, AND HOBBIES FROM AROUND THE WORLD TO INSPIRE YOUR NEXT CHAPTER

RAVINA M CHANDRA

RMC PUBLISHERS

Published by RMC Publishers

ISBN 978-1-7782681-3-7 (Paperback)
ISBN 978-1-7780029-9-1 (E-book)

www.ravinachandra.com

This book is dedicated to you, dad.

Always been inspired by your keen sense of curiosity and pursuit of hobbies throughout your entire life. You are actively gardening, working on woodworking projects (like raised-gardening beds and gardening signs), setting up automatic watering systems, re-covering chairs, and the list goes on.

It's truly a privilege being your daughter.

ALSO BY RAVINA M CHANDRA

In the *Inspired Retirement Living* Series

101 Ways to Enjoy Retirement
101 Ways to Enjoy Retirement Across America

Other books

The Art of Senior Dating
Longevity and Eating Habits
My Vibrant Life

YOUR FREE GIFT

I'd like to offer you a gift to say thank you for purchasing this book. Here is a booklet for creating your perfect Morning Routine for better productivity, lowering stress, and developing healthy habits.

In '**4 Simple Steps to Create Your Perfect Morning Routine**,' you will learn:

• What a **morning routine** is and why it is essential

• The secret of creating a morning routine using these **four components** that will **align with your core values**

• How a morning routine can elevate your life so that you may live **vibrantly,** no matter if you are a student, working, or retired

Go to www.RavinaChandra.com/books to get it NOW!

TABLE OF CONTENTS

INTRODUCTION

Retirement – at last.

The days are long and full of promise. But how do you fill them? How do you spend your long-awaited freedom?

Retiring opens the door to a bewildering range of activities you never had time for before. This book looks at ways people enjoy their hobbies in 21 countries around the world. You will find many hobbies you are familiar with and some that are new to you. Some you will pass by quickly, but others you might find intriguing.

When Fran retired from a busy life managing a retail company, she decided to put her feet up, rest, relax – and do absolutely nothing.

This lasted for a whole ten days!

She was bored and lonely and didn't think life had anything left to offer her. But, as John Kennedy famously said in his

inaugural speech on becoming president of the United States –
"Think not what your country can do for you – think what you
can do for your country."

Fran remembered these words as she watched yet another old
TV series, which was a wake-up call. That night she felt
excited, and her brain felt like it was going round and round in
circles. Sleep just wouldn't come.

She knew she had to get some order into her life and realized it
was down to her to go out and join in the social life around her.
It was down to her to find interesting hobbies that challenged
her. She knew she had an excellent opportunity to learn new
skills, make new friends, and live each day fully and
completely.

Keeping your interest in our wonderful world alive, is the
best way to stay fit physically, but also mentally. People
who socialize, take some form of exercise and stimulate
their brains, by learning new things, are the ones who are
happy in their later years.

Cooking is becoming increasingly popular, and you will
find some delicious recipes to try out, share, and delight
your friends and family. There are many other ways to use
your creative skills: some you may already do, some you
may have tried as a child, and some will be unexpected.

While you probably won't be advised to participate in
combative sports like wrestling and boxing, for example,
there are plenty of physical activities to keep you supple
and fit. And you can always watch a football match and
cheer your team on.

Age brings wisdom and a wealth of knowledge to our brains. It is a time when we can catch up on everything we never had time for. As you read this book, you will find the days are filled with excitement, and now you have time to appreciate and enjoy it.

My entire career has been in healthcare, and much of my time has been spent with older clients, who are often inspiring, unique, and always interesting. Engaging with them has stimulated my own life in so many ways.

I am hoping this book will help to enrich your life, even a very tiny bit. So, stay curious, stay adventurous, and dive in.

One more thing to mention before you delve into the pages of this book, as I know some of you are wondering why your country is missing.

For every chapter of this book, thorough research and interviews took place to ensure proper representation of hobbies and countries. First, check if your country was featured in my first hobbies book. If not, and you would like your country or hobby featured in an upcoming book, I would love to hear from you. A special shout-out to my American friends. What a vast and diverse country you have. Coming shortly is your very own, special edition of 101 Hobbies from Across the U.S.A.

Please get in touch with me with your ideas at:
ravina@ravinachandra.com

INDIA

The people of India (Indians) seem able to absorb cultures from all over the world. Like much of the world, modern hobbies include reading, social media, streaming television, and playing video games. Indians also enjoy the hobby of design creation, such as graphic design, excelling at this on a professional level too.

While reading might seem old-fashioned, the younger generation enjoys reading fiction – favoring fantasy, romance, and thrillers. Older people prefer non-fiction, including self-help, health, and business.

Indian residents were surveyed regarding what drives them and their passions. It was discovered that Indians take their leisure time seriously, with twenty-percent spending at least an hour a day on hobbies. In addition, three-quarters of the population spend a quarter of their salary on hobbies—a good life-work balance.

But there are some things that the Indian population are particularly good at. They also use their hobbies to make friends, and we know that good social interaction is excellent for our health. The hobbies I have chosen to represent India are a nice mixture of physically stimulating and mentally relaxing.

KITE FLYING

Uttarayan – the International Kite Festival, is primarily a Hindu festival that celebrates the day the sun transits into the Northern hemisphere and into the sign of Capricorn. This is the day known as Makar Sankranti – on the 14th of January or the 15th, depending on if it's a leap year. In the state of Gujarat and some other states in India, this is a two-day public holiday. It is one of the biggest festivals in India.

Makar Sankranti is when the gods awaken from their deep winter sleep.

The Rigged is an ancient Indian collection of Vedic Sanskrit hymns and mentions the festival 5,000 years ago. The Rigveda derives from the words for praise and knowledge and is one of four sacred Hindu texts known as the 'Vedas,' among the oldest surviving texts in any Indo-European language.

The ancient kings and Nawabs enjoyed the sport of kite flying, but now anyone can fly their kite – and people come from all over the world to revel in the entertainment.

People start preparing many weeks in advance. Apart from the kites, there are fine clothes and costumes to make and festive foods to prepare. It's an exciting time for the young and the old.

Throughout the kite flying week, the markets are full of colorful kites and all the accessories you could possibly want to enjoy this spectacle. In Gujarat, the town of Ahmedabad has one of the largest markets, and at the nearby riverfront, you might find up to 500,000 people, many lying down to watch the kites filling the skies overhead.

Kites come in various shapes and sizes, often influenced by their country of origin. For example, from Italy comes sculptured kites, from Japan comes fighting kites, and from China the spectacular dragon kites.

People make kites from many different materials – plastic, leaves, nylon, metal, wood, and an assortment of scrap materials. But the true Uttarayan kites are made from bamboo and lightweight paper. Most are rhomboid in shape, with a central spine and one bow. The kites are often brightly painted; a tiger may have stripes, and a dragon fiery breath.

You do not want to get in the way of the lines, either. They are commonly covered with glue and ground glass. After drying, they are rolled up and attached to the back of the kite and are called 'firkees' – razor-sharp. These 'patangs,' or fighter kites, are used to cut down the opponents' kites. Kite battles can be a cutthroat business!

If you want to make your own kite, they are not too hard to make – and you can decorate it in any way pleasing to you. Children or grandchildren may be keen to help. And flying can be exhilarating, out in the wind watching your creation sing up into the skies.

You can also buy readymade kits if you don't want to make them from scratch. Kite flying can be a friendly hobby – and once you have successfully flown your kite, you will want to do it again and again.

INDIAN CURRY MAKING

Curry is one of the most popular foods worldwide – but nothing can beat a good Indian curry.

India is a big country, so it is not surprising that there are an almost infinite number of local variations and seasonal varieties of curry. Everywhere you go in India, you can find exciting and nutritious curries. And of the eighty different spices worldwide – fifty are grown in India – they have hundreds of years of experience in their use.

Simple foods like potatoes can be turned into tasty and exotic dishes with the skillful use of herbs and spices.

Here is a list of ingredients for a spicy potato curry that runs something like this:

Potatoes
Onion
Tomatoes
Chili powder
Cumin seeds
Sprig of curry leaves
Ginger
Garlic
Salt
Turmeric
Coriander
Garam masala
Red chili powder

Optional:
Coconut milk
Mustard seeds
Bay leaf

Herbs and spices can make a dish taste delicious – many herbs and spices are also credited with medicinal properties. So, let us look at some of the most commonly used ingredients in Indian curry. Small changes in spices can create original and very different-tasting curries.

Apart from onions, cilantro, tomatoes, vegetable oils, and ginger, the common spices used are curry powder, turmeric, cayenne pepper, cloves, cardamom, fenugreek, and cumin.

What properties are credited to some of these spices?

Turmeric

Turmeric has a reputation as an anti-inflammatory, and we are beginning to recognize just how important this property is for our health and longevity. Turmeric treats arthritis and other inflammatory diseases and improves our immune system.

Cumin

Cumin is claimed to relieve toothaches and prevent certain diseases because of its antioxidant properties.

Fenugreek

Fenugreek is known to lower blood sugar levels in people with diabetes and help preserve food.

Coriander

Rich in immune-boosting antioxidants, coriander is good for coughs, allergies, and skin rashes. It also helps thicken gravy – and the fresh leaves make a delightful garnish.

Cloves

Cloves have been used for many years for their pain-relieving benefits to help tooth pain. In addition, some use cloves to ease digestive problems by brewing tea with cloves and ginger.

Cardamon

Cardamon may lower blood pressure due to its diuretic effect, promoting urination and removing water that builds up in your body. Using cardamon to treat bad breath and improve oral health has been an ancient remedy for years.

Cooking a curry can be mentally stimulating, not too tricky, and very rewarding. In addition, it is a great way to entertain guests, making it a wonderful hobby your friends will be pleased about.

MANDALA DRAWING

People from many countries have created mandalas. Often this is in the religious context but sometimes simply for the pleasure of creating a beautiful and ordered design. You can find them in Australian aborigines' cultures, Aztec civilizations, and Catholic Christianity.

The most common religions in the world are Christianity, Islam, and thirdly Hinduism, and about 80% of the Indian population are Hindus. But India is home to many other religions, including Islam, Christianity, Buddhism, Sikhs, and Jains.

Hinduism might be the oldest major religion globally and can be traced back 5,000 years or more – and mandalas are closely associated with Hindu and Buddhist meditations and art.

Mandalas serve as a guided pathway to enlightenment. They represent the universe and act as an aid to meditation, self-awareness, and finding one's way in the grand scheme of life.

The traditional mandala is circular in shape, symmetrical, and colored. Sometimes the circle is placed with a square with four T-shaped gates. It represents purity and enlightenment. Or it might represent the entire universe, with a sacred mountain in the center and the continents around it.

Mandalas may be used for teaching, healing, or as a guide to inner consciousness. They can help focus one's attention, clear distracting thoughts from the mind, and act as a map representing the gods in some religions. One works through the mandala from the outer edges to the central core.

The great thing about mandalas is that you can produce your own and give it an inner meaning right for you. Creating your mandala is also very relaxing, and many adult coloring books feature mandalas.

Mandalas can be drawn on paper or silk or made into wall hangings or rugs – even patchwork creations for quilts or throws. Whatever your skills are, a mandala can be a relaxing and instructive skill.

DESIGN AND MOOD BOARD CREATION

Indians love color and design, so it's no surprise that illustration and design are increasingly popular hobbies. Many of the best professional designers are Indians.

There are so many applications for your designs. For example, you may use it to make a book cover, cover cardboard boxes to make stylish storage containers, infographics on the internet, or perhaps design your clothing.

The idea behind graphic design is to make a visual representation of your thoughts. It can increase clarity in your mind, help you see the way through problems, and be an excellent way to communicate your ideas.

Fortunately, many online courses help you with your digital design start-up. If you do not want to use computers, you can still make a mood board with pictures, colors, and a little writing in different styles. Making a collage of your ideas can look attractive and help you sort out your mind.

Learning to make online digital designs takes effort and research – but the results can be remarkable. And one of the best things is that you can share your results with people on the other side of the world if you wish.

Mood Boards

A mood board is one way to put your ideas together visually, perhaps before creating your final design or simply as an attractive way to organize your thoughts.

It is easy to change the mood board as your ideas align with your new aspirations. Your mood board is a very personal thing – they can come in many guises – different shapes – different color co-ordinations – different styles.

Some things of note might be images like stock photos, personal memoirs, or drawings. Colors can help coordinate your theme, arrows can lead you from one part to another, and words can be in color, attractive fonts, and large enough to have an impact. Textures can be used for good effect, on-screen or in materials if your collage is physical.

But if you need help with this, you can find templates on the internet. For example, photoshop and Canva are well worth exploring. Instagram and Pinterest are just two sites where you might find a few ideas. Mood boards are fun to make, and creating your designs can be addictive.

SUMMARY

India is a vast continent with a huge variety of natural scenery, the second largest population globally, and many different outlooks on life. Yet they seem able to assimilate other cultures and adapt them to suit themselves.

Kite Flying
Curry Making
Mandela Drawing
Design and Mood Board Creation

SWEDEN

Sweden is the largest country in Northern Europe. It has massive forests, high mountains, and a long coastline with thousands of islands. Did you know that the capital city, Stockholm, is built on 14 islands and has over 50 bridges!

Sweden has long dark days in winter, encouraging Swedes to find indoor hobbies – so reading, playing games with family and friends, or putting around on the internet are popular hobbies.

Moderation in all things is a way of life in Sweden, which is reflected in their interior decorating. They have a world-wide reputation for clean lines and fuss-free furniture and homes. Crafts, music, and cooking are hobbies enjoyed by Sweden's people. I have picked out some hobbies that identify with their philosophy of life and their thoughtfulness for other people. So, let's have a look.

LAGOM

Lagom means 'just the right amount,' 'in balance,' 'suitable,' and so on...

The earliest examples are to be found in 17th-century texts. The word comes from 'lag' for 'law' or 'according to custom.' It has been suggested that the word 'lagom' is a contraction of 'laget om,' which means 'around the team' and is said to relate to how much mead one should drink from the Viking horn as it was passed around the hall so that all would be able to drink a fair share. A nice idea but probably not entirely true.

But as mentioned, the idea of moderation is an integral part of Swedish culture. Enough is as good as a feast. Greed and the accumulation of things you do not need are alien to most Swedes. Why have ten toothbrushes when you only use one at a time?

Other countries may have similar ideas with slightly different emphases. For example, just right, comfortable, or fine is another way of expressing how things seem and how you feel. Some countries with specific words for this idea of moderation include Norway, Finland, Albania, and Thailand. Even the ancient Greeks had a phrase meaning 'moderation is best.'

Maybe you are already a 'lagom' sort of person? If not, would taking on this concept be a good hobby for you? For example, decluttering your home environment over a period of time or aiming for a more minimalist attitude and existence might give you lagom.

There are various online programs to help with this way of life. It does tie into the Swedish character of 'enough is enough' and makes for a streamlined quality of life.

COFFEE CULTURE IN SWEDEN

'Fika' is a Swedish form of taking a coffee break, and always with a pastry or other snack. What better way to relax with your family and friends? It's not just a coffee with a to-go cup; it's a time to slow down and gather with friends or a moment on your own to reflect on your day.

In 2017, the Telegraph claimed that Swedes consumed more coffee than most other nations. The estimate was 8.2 kg per person per year. Since the early 1800s, coffee drinking has been part of the way of life for Swedes, and there is no sign of slowing down.

Any time of day will do; you do not need an excuse to drink coffee. But 11 a.m. is perhaps the favorite time to settle down with a cinnamon or cardamon bun and a cup of coffee. Many Swedes take a second Fika break later in the afternoon, around 3 p.m., especially if they work in an office environment.

So entrenched is the coffee culture that local bakeries have started opening up the front of their shops to form small cafes with fresh buns. This ritual certainly propels you to pause your busy day.

LÖRDAGSGODIS

Too much of a good thing palls, so a treat on Saturdays is something children can look forward to and enjoy. Adults with a sweet tooth can also look forward to an enjoyable part of their weekly routine.

'Lördagsgodis' means 'Saturday sweets or candy.' Since the 1950s, this has become a part of Swedish culture. They say that a little of what you like is good for you. And this applies to small quantities of sweets.

Sweets, as you know, contain sugar, are not great for your teeth, and incline people to obesity. As the country became wealthier, people had more to spend on treats. To limit increasing rates of tooth decay, the Swedish medical authorities recommended limiting sweets to once a week.

Swedish sweets generally do not contain trans fats, high-fructose corn syrup, or gluten, making them less harmful than candy that does include these ingredients.

One of the favorite Swedish treats is called Skumkantareller – which translates as Foam Mushrooms. They are shaped like mushrooms, are soft and chewy, and taste nothing like mushrooms.

Apart from the health benefits of limiting sweets, this Lördagsgodis teaches children (and adults!) to wait, plan ahead, and instill a little self-discipline. Maybe you have something a little 'naughty' you enjoy eating? Perhaps you would enjoy it even more if you limited it to just one day a week?

You could turn your hobby of making bread or pastries, for example, into a memorable event once a week or once a month.

SWEDISH SAUNA

Saunas in Sweden are often used as a great way to relax, even though Finland is where saunas are most used. There are a huge number of saunas in Sweden – often known as 'bastu.' Many are found in leisure centers, spas, and swimming pools.

Spas are very popular, and the tradition of a hot sauna followed by an icy dip, and maybe a wonderful Swedish massage could untie any knots in your muscles and make you feel on top of the world.

In the fifth century, saunas were found in shallow caves on the mountainsides. There you would find a hot stove with heated stones. As the water was poured into the rocks, steam rose, and the humidity increased – and so did the feeling of heat.

Then wooden buildings with iron stoves came into being. Mothers often gave birth in one of these saunas because they were immaculate, and post-natal infection was unlikely to occur. In the 18th century, saunas were considered hotbeds of immoral behaviors and outlawed. It was thought that they also encouraged the spread of syphilis.

The etiquette is simple, you enter naked but wrapped in a towel. In fact, the towel is essential to sit on. You must shower beforehand, and food and drink are not usually allowed in the sauna. It's just a matter of good manners. Sometimes the sexes are segregated but not generally, as nudity is generally well accepted by the Swedes.

Today, saunas are not only an excellent way to relax but are also known for their health benefits, including releasing toxins from your body, soothing aching muscles, and reducing inflammation.

For many tourists, a Swedish sauna is on their bucket list. But you could always make a habit of sauna use by purchasing one for your home or checking whether there are any in your local area. If buying a sauna is too much for you, another option is an infrared sauna blanket which is inexpensive and easy to use. Please do your sauna research, though, as there are many different makes and models, so find out what is best for you.

DÖSTÄDNING

'Dö' is death in Swedish, and 'städning' means standing or cleaning. You can also call it 'death cleaning.'

Times change. All those things you thought your grand-children would want – maybe they don't. You likely want to make your passing as easy for your family as possible, which means getting rid of the things you no longer enjoy and those things you can be reasonably sure your family won't want.

Family may want mementos; they may want photographs, even personal things you might have written or crafted, special recipes, and maybe your gardening tools. But they probably do not want your old clothes you no longer wear or that malfunctioning kitchen apparatus.

It is so easy to accumulate STUFF. But you will eventually die like everyone else. Death and taxes, as they say, are the only sure things in life. Your loved ones will most likely be upset and sad when you die. So, make it easier for them.

Does this feel like work instead of a hobby? Maybe for some. But once you get into döstädning, gradually getting rid of things you don't get pleasure from, giving them away, sending them to charity, or throwing them out, you may feel better having freed yourself from clutter. So keep the things you love, and jettison the rest. It's your last gift to your family.

You may find pleasure in going through items hidden away untouched for years. You may feel virtuous when you can give your 'junk' to a charity. You may enjoy giving a surprise gift to a friend.

Death cleaning isn't about dusting and tidying up; it can be seen as a permanent way of organizing your life. It takes courage to face the fact that none of us are immortal. Getting rid of excess allows us to focus on what we appreciate.

SUMMARY

Swedes have found a good life/work balance. Moderation in all things seems to be their standard, and the civilized coffee culture is an excellent example of this. So, too, is the lördagsgodis – a perfect way to have something to look forward to but not to indulge in excess.

'Just enough' links the things Swedes live by, but maybe the sauna is an exception. Death clearing sounds a bit sad but is a way to enjoy the things that matter and to help the people you love after your death.

Lagom
Coffee culture
Lördagsgodis
Sauna
Döstädning

IRELAND (ÉIRE)

T he 'Emerald Isle' is green and stunningly beautiful, and the people are full of character.

There has been some confusion about what to call this country. The island is divided – the smaller part, Ulster, in the north, is part of Great Britain. The rest of the island is known as Ireland in English or Éire and is entirely independent.

In 1949, Éire left the Commonwealth and became a republic. The legend tells us that one of the Tuath Dé Danann ('tribe of Gods') named Ernmas had nine children, six of whom were daughters. Three of these became goddesses: Ériu, Banba, and Fódla. Ireland is derived from the name Ériu. In old Irish, this means 'abundant land.'

The land is green, often boggy, with rugged hills and sea cliffs. There are many small islets and inlets on the western shore. It is known to be rainy and misty – hence

⅃ around the landscape are archeological
s, and ancient castles.

‿hristianised early and produced some of the
‿ᴐᴦ beautiful medieval religious books. Around 73% of
the population are Catholics today. And Irish pubs are
featured worldwide. Sports such as football, golf, and
rugby are popular – but Ireland is well known for horse
racing and some more local sports like hurling and Gaelic
football.

I have chosen five hobbies for you to explore, so let's look
at them.

IRISH FAIRIES AND LEPRECHAUNS

Ireland is a land of myths and magic. The soft green of the
hills, the crashing Atlantic Ocean on its western shores,
and the ever-present myths and legends make Ireland
seem a mystical place.

Ireland has its own Gaelic language and Celtic heritage.
Keeping the myths alive was an oral tradition. People
gathered around the fireside, telling the tales of long ago,
perhaps accompanied by a small harp. These tales have
been handed down for hundreds of years, almost word for
word.

In the 11th century, Irish monks were recording these tales
and helping to keep alive the Celtic mythology – Catholi-
cism and 'fairy faith' can co-exist in harmony. The harp of
Dagda is just one of many Irish legends. Dagda was a
famous warrior and chieftain who owned a magic harp.

He was of the tall, golden-haired, and blue-eyed people from the north, suggesting a Viking ancestry.

What else is featured in these tales? Heroes and battles, but also banshees, fairies, and leprechauns. The banshee is a female fairy in both Irish and Scots Gaelic. If you heard the banshee wailing, prepare for the death of a family member.

But perhaps the best-known Irish fairy is the leprechaun. They have various forms and modes of dress. They are generally depicted as small and solitary men bent on mischief. But, dressed in red or green, with a fine beard, they might be shown as shoe-makers, or maybe they have hidden a pot of gold at the end of the rainbow?

One medieval tale tells of King Fergus who fell asleep on the beach. He woke up being dragged into the sea by three leprechauns. He captured them and only let them go in exchange for three wishes.

Various sports teams use leprechauns as mascots – and a wrestler called Dylan Mark Postl competed under the name of a leprechaun called Hornswoggle.

You may not have a leprechaun in your backyard, but there might be local myths and legends that would be interesting to research. If not, why not read about Irish folklore, which is full of adventure, and perhaps you will come to believe in the fairies yourself?

WATERCOLOR PAINTING

Ireland is incredibly beautiful and lends itself to the soft washes of watercolor painting.

Known as the 'Emerald Isle,' one tends to imagine a million shades of green, but when you look and see, you will notice hundreds of blues and other colors. Even in the rain and mist, color and a sense of mystique are part of Ireland's charm.

Because watercolors are transparent, they are often laid down in layers. And if you want a soft, blending effect, then wet-on-wet might be your chosen method. You could use wet-on-dry, dry-on-dry, and dry-on-wet. The paper you use will also affect the finished effect.

There are many videos to demonstrate how to paint watercolors, and looking at the efforts of Irish painters might stimulate you to try your hand. The lovely scenery and delicate colors of Éire have encouraged many people to try capturing some of this island's atmosphere. Watercolor painting is one hobby that is engrossing and can be very satisfying.

SODA BREAD BAKING

Ireland suffered from a devastating potato famine from 1845 to 1849. Soda bread was one alternative food for the poverty-stricken people. Imagine them baking it over their turf fires in their small cottages. It is easy to make, filling, and very tasty.

The Irish eat soda bread for breakfast with jam and a cup of tea. They eat it for lunch with cheese and for dinner with the entrée. But the very best way to eat it is straight from the oven while it is still warm, with salty butter or a big dollop of jam.

What is so special about soda bread? Instead of yeast as the rising agent in soda bread, it uses sodium bicarbonate.

Traditional Irish soda

Traditional soda bread has just four ingredients: flour, baking soda, buttermilk, and salt.

Some modern bakers may add Guinness, orange peel, or other things, but that deviates from the real soda bread, although it may taste delicious.

The taste of the bread comes from the way the baking soda and acidic milk react to form tiny carbon dioxide bubbles in the bread. This gives it a unique texture. And you do not need to knead it, so it is quick to make.

Here is a recipe for you to try:

Ingredients

170 g (6 oz) wholemeal flour and 170 g (6 oz) plain flour
½ tsp salt
½ tsp bicarbonate of soda
290 ml (10 fl oz) buttermilk

Method

- Preheat the oven to 200°C (390°F).
- Put all the dry ingredients in a bowl, make a well in the center, and pour in the buttermilk.
- Mix with a fork to form a soft dough. Adjust the quantity of milk if necessary.
- Turn out onto a floured surface and form into a round shape. Lightly flour a baking sheet and place the slightly-flattened dough on it. Mark a cross on the surface.
- Bake in a hot oven for about 30 minutes.
- It should sound hollow when you tap it. Cool on a wire rack.

Soda bread is delicious. Try it and see! If you are in a hurry and have unexpected guests, this takes about an hour to make and cook and is an unusual and filling offering. Why not make two loaves?

IRISH COMEDY

Irish people have an irresistible sense of humor. It's light, funny, and not offensive.

Often the humor depends upon wordplay and inverted meaning. The punchline will often tell how one person outwits another or confuses him. There is a topsy-turvy logic, which is quite delightful.

When the English imposed their language on the Irish, speaking traditional Irish Gaelic was forbidden, so the

Irish people spoke English the Irish way. Unfortunately, many grammatical rules of English are the reverse of Gaelic rules, resulting in an inversion of the language. In addition, any logic was abandoned as being too foolish or abstract for words.

The traditional oral storytellers often had stories with a twist in the tale, which lends itself to modern Irish humor. It can be subtle and only appreciated when you hear the joke delivered in the soft Irish brogue. And nearly all Irish people can tell a funny tale– it seems to come as a natural part of their makeup. Sometimes, you might have to be Irish to 'get it,' though.

Maybe you have a stock of jokes to access when you meet with friends or grandchildren. As a hobby, telling jokes and riddles can be a great way to communicate intergenerationally. They also say that a good belly laugh is one of the very best stress relievers we have.

DUCK HERDING

Dogs herd sheep – yes? But they can also herd other animals - such as ducks. This isn't quite as quaint as it sounds. How else can you put your ducks safely inside a locked pen at night to deprive foxes and other predators?

Some dogs are not much good at herding anything, but others are natural herders. This can be a problem if you are hill walking with your dog and sheep are around. You may think they may be on the next hill, far away, until you see a tiny black and white animal running fast behind a flock of sheep.

Dogs need to be trained for herding, and so do their owners. Some dogs know what a duck looks like, sounds like, and runs like. They recognize the job they have to do in herding the ducks to safety when the farmer commands them to.

A well-trained dog with an aptitude for herding can be taught to herd hens, ducks, and sheep. These dogs need to be gentle, intelligent, and sensitive to the farmer's commands and how the ducks respond. Not all dogs are suitable for duck-herding. But some well-trained dogs do work on a few farms in Ireland.

Watching them spring into action is engaging and quite awe-inspiring.

If you do not have dogs of your own, you can watch them in action at shows or in videos. And if you have a natural couch dog, you can show him too. You might decide to work with your dog to train him in herding. What you can't do is take your dog to the nearest hills and let him or her off the lead and expect them to understand how to act. But it is an entertaining activity to watch.

SUMMARY

Ireland might be a small country, but it has stunning scenery and a wide variety of activities to offer. One cannot think about Éire without thinking about legends and myths.

The misty landscape lends itself to the transparent paints of watercolors, and painting is an engrossing hobby with easy access to how-to videos and classes. And if that makes you hungry, soda bread is a fast way to satisfy your appetite. The Irish are funny. Humor is in their genes, and everyone can enjoy a good laugh. Finally, the gentle sport of duck herding – anyone can watch or join in under guidance.

Irish fairies and leprechauns
Watercolor painting
Soda bread baking
Comedy
Duck herding

MONGOLIA

Mongolia is cold and dry. The vast Gobi Desert stretches across large parts of Mongolia and China. The name means "waterless place" in Mongolian. You need strong and tough people to thrive in this harsh climate.

Genghis Khan was a renowned warrior, his hordes sweeping westward across central Asia and southeastward over the Great Wall of China. Today many people still have a nomadic lifestyle – and their hobbies are those needed to survive, like archery or horse and camel racing. Hobbies that are portable and weigh very little such as their wire and ankle bone games are also popular.

These games help pass the frigid winter evenings and involve all ages of the families, who tend to live together in small communities sharing work and play.

They have Naadam, a yearly festival celebrating three traditional games: wrestling, archery, and horse racing. These traditional games are unique, and I have chosen five to represent the variety of Mongolian games and hobbies.

WIRE PUZZLE GAMES

Mongolian puzzle games have been around for a very long time. They were probably played in the Xiongnu, when the Xiongnu were nomads who dominated the Asian steppes, including what is now Mongolia, for over 500 years around the 3rd century BC.

Mongolia has created some of the world's most challenging puzzles and sets. They have nearly 3,000 games of 15 sorts inherited from their ancestors. They are said to help a child's intellectual development.

The games exercise memory, logical thinking, concentration, and problem-solving skills, all needed for the nomadic lifestyle in harsh terrain. There are many puzzle games and variations of wire puzzles.

The golden key wire toy is one such puzzle. This is an iron key ring game. The aim is to unlock as many ring locks without any tools. Sometimes our Christmas crackers may have a small wire escape toy inside – but these are nothing like the complexity of the Mongolian Golden Key.

The puzzles or nail puzzles usually consist of two or more wires tangled up. Closed pieces may include rings or other shapes. So, again, untangle it without cutting the wires or bending them.

These games can be homemade from nails, horseshoes, or any metal. Another variation is a plate and ring puzzle. This has a plate with lots of holes drilled in it and a closed or nearly closed ring that must be disentangled from the plate. You can buy these puzzles with instructions on how to solve them, but they can be complex even with instructions. What a simple yet challenging hobby to work your brain.

ANKLE BONE GAMES

The name for an ankle bone game in Mongolian is 'Shagai,' and there are many, many games played using the ankle bones of goats or sheep. Games similar to dice, games of fortune-telling, and flicking.

These games such as multicolored turtle, flicking, and knucklebones, have strict rules.

One of the most popular games is Alag Malkhii, the multicolored turtle. This game is believed to bring luck to families. According to Buddhist beliefs, the numbers 81 and 108 are lucky, so the number of bones used is 81 or 108.

The bones are painted in five different colors and put in the shape of a turtle (which represents the shape of the Universe). Then, players roll the dice and collect the bones to make their own little turtle. The winner is the player who has created the most turtles when all the bones have been used.

You will be glad to know that the bones are cleaned and polished before use. The bones have four sides, although they are naturally irregular. I am not sure what your local butcher would make of a request for ankle bones, but you can buy sets of them. Working out the ways to play would be an interesting and unusual hobby.

BUILD YOUR OWN YURT

You can build your own yurt, any size, from a miniature toy to a live-in tent size. The yurt is the Mongolian prefabricated and removable house – a luxurious tent with windows and door frames.

The traditional yurt is called a "ger" and differs only in the roof construction. They have been in existence for over 300 years, so they are much tested. As a nomadic house, the yurts are quick to erect and withstand the winds. They are light to carry and essential since Mongolian nomads tended to move locations four or more times a year.

Building your own yurt, whether it be a miniature model or a nearly full size, helps us to understand a little of the culture of these unique nomadic people. Many are highly decorated and beautifully constructed. You can buy kits of all sizes for your grandchildren and yourself. Model yurt building would make an informative and unusual hobby.

ARCHERY

Archery in Mongolia has an important place in past legends and history. Erekhe Mergen was a famous archer. When there was a terrible drought, he saved the people by shooting down no less than six suns.

The legendary 'Mother of Mongolia' wanted to make peace between her aggressive sons. So she gave each son an arrow and told them to break it. That was easy! Then she gave each son a bunch of six arrows and told them to snap it – and they couldn't. The lesson? In unity is strength.

Then came Genghis Khan and his horde of Huns sweeping across vast areas of Asia, with their hardy mares and bows, cutting down all in their path. The bows of Genghis Khan were smaller than modern bows but very effective. Did you know that his military conquests were not the only way Genghis Khan imprinted his fame on the world? It is said that there are 16 million men who might be directly descended from him! They have the same Y chromosome.

Archery was essential to the Mongolian nomadic life to obtain food. Children grew up learning to use the bow and arrow from a young age. Archery is still a popular hobby, and there are Mongolian archery festivals. These are colorful affairs with hundreds of white gers and multi-colored tents spread across the ground. The composite bow can take a long time to create from natural materials.

Archery is a hobby that we can all enjoy – although the Mongolian method might be hard to emulate.

DEMBEE

Dembee is a finger game with elements of chanting, visual acuity, and manual dexterity.

The idea is to guess the number of fingers two players are displaying. But the game is fast and furious. The fingers move quickly, so you must respond at speed – in a sing-song manner – cantillating. Every time you score, you press one finger on one hand, and the first to reach the fifth finger wins.

The penalty for losing is to drink fermented (sour) milk.

This game tests all your senses – vision, hearing, response speed, fingers' agility, and even taste if you lose. So, you guess and tell, almost like a musical debate. To make it more demanding, the fingers have names such as 'Spick one' and 'seven Domboo.'

This is a demanding game, and variations in how the fingers are shown, or the melodies used, make it constantly exciting and testing.

Dembee is a traditional game derived from the ancient custom of starting to milk the mares at the beginning of summer and making fermented milk. And anyone can play – young or old, man or woman. But every loser must drink the 'airag' to the bottom of the cup. Otherwise, severe weather would follow. They even have a special bowl for drinking the airag – and the fermented mare's milk has many medicinal properties.

To play Dembee, you would need to watch, either on video or, if lucky, the real experience. One advantage of this game is that you need nothing except your acute senses to play - except the airag.

SUMMARY

Mongolia has a significant number of unique games suited to its nomadic lifestyle and harsh climate. It is a fascinating country, and playing their games helps us understand a little about their lives.

Wire Puzzles Games
Anklebone Games
Build your Own Yurt
Archery
Dembee

SOUTH KOREA

South Koreans know how to work hard and play hard. The working week was reduced from 68 hours maximum to 52 hours in 2018, giving people more opportunities to enjoy their hobbies.

The most popular hobbies for South Koreans concern fitness and sport (34%), according to a survey carried out in 2019. This was followed by learning a foreign language (28%) and learning how to invest in third (24%).

Some of the sports enjoyed include badminton, football, baseball, and traditional martial arts like Taekwondo and judo – the former being extremely energetic, with kicks and fast movements taking a lifetime to become proficient. Many South Koreans are now taking up fencing and enjoying its competitiveness.

South Korea has some beautiful natural parks to explore. Of course, music plays an integral part in social life. But learning a foreign language, very often English, is seen as almost essential with the increased use of the internet and social media.

Let's dive into the most popular hobbies a South Korean is likely to partake in.

HIKING

Hiking is a popular hobby in South Korea – and there is good reason for this. The countryside is gorgeous, and the hard-working people of South Korea likely crave a change of scenery for some mental relaxation.

Apart from the green hilly countryside, cherry trees, and ancient Buddhist temples, there are sub-tropical islands to explore and the coastline with its fishing villages.

The Seoraksan National Park has been a UNESCO Biosphere Protection site since 1982. Covering 63 square miles, it has many places to discover. There are lovely mountains like Seoraksan Mountain, or 'Snowy Mountain,' reaching 5,604 ft high. Beautiful mountain trails and stunning scenery, including steep cliffs, waterfalls, and caves.

The Sinheunga is reputed to be the oldest Seon temple in the world. Surrounding the temple complex are around 200 pools. And if animals interest you, there are otters, flying squirrels, maybe a black bear, and if you are fortunate, you might catch a glimpse of the rare Korean musk deer or Korean goral.

There are national parks and pleasant countryside near most of us – and the thing is - when we live in a particular place, we are less likely to hike around and explore the natural wonders near home. So why not list the spectacular sites nearby and take the time to hike and explore locally?

FOLK MUSIC

In 1145, the history of the three kingdoms described two stringlike instruments. Music reflected the social hierarchy. The elite classes used orthodox music, usually played in ceremonies, banquets, and military processions. And then there was the people's music, which included folk songs, becoming increasingly respected as the traditional music of South Korea.

Pansori, meaning 'the place where many people gather,' originated in the 17th century – perhaps derived from the shamanic narrative song. Pansori music contains percussion and a solo singer, the contemporary music of South Korea. Pungmul Nori is percussion music with dominant drums and is considered traditional music. Folk songs varied from region to region.

When Japan overcame the Korean peninsula in 1895, they imposed a European style of music, but this was less accessible to the poorer classes, and they maintained their traditional style of music. For example, you may know the song, 'Oh, my darling Clementine?' This derives from the modern Ch'angga, which in turn comes from Pansori. So as you can see, South Korean music has a complex past and combines traditional Korean music and ballads with Western styles. And now we have 'K-pop' with large boy bands who sing and dance. This may or may not be your style, but it is undoubtedly easy to sing along with.

Folk music is a music style still found worldwide and has quite the following, with folk festivals cropping up all over the place. If you enjoy this music and are drawn to this sound, why not make a hobby of it. Listening to it or picking up an instrument like a guitar and creating your own folk songs are great choices.

FENCING

The number one hobby for South Koreans is keeping physically fit with a sports activity, and the most up-and-coming sport is fencing.

South Korean fencers have won five gold medals, three silver, and eight bronze medals in Olympic fencing as of the time of writing – and alongside China, this is the most for any Asian country.

The men's saber team have interesting names: 'The Terminator,' 'The Legend,' and 'The Sonic.' One is left-handed, which must have its advantages. Their leader is number eight in the world ranking. This is an exceptional achievement since fencing has been a European sport until quite recently.

Gaining in popularity in South Korea, you will be able to note the progression of South Korea in fencing, and it is a fun sport to watch with its grace and fast moves.

Maybe there is a team near you or a club you could participate in? Fencing is a sport open to men and women – and while a specific strength and dexterity are needed, it also depends upon strategy. It could be compared to a physical form of chess.

Fencing would be quite a demanding sport, but if you are reasonably fit, it gives an excellent workout for the body and the brain at any age.

FOREIGN LANGUAGE LEARNING

Learning a foreign language is the second most popular leisure-time activity in South Korea, and it is also one suggested method to stave off dementia.

In Korea, the most common foreign language learned is English (the language of business.) Mandarin and Japanese are also in demand. South Koreans are very competitive, and speaking English is one way to advance. Entrance to Universities demands a high proficiency in English, plus the fact that much of the internet language is predominantly English.

And how about you?

If you want to learn a new language do you want to become proficient quickly, do you want a real challenge, or have you some practical purpose in mind?

To help you make up your mind, here are some 'easier' languages for English speakers:

Norwegian has many similar words, straightforward grammar, and so many local accents that you don't need to worry about pronunciation.

Spanish also has many similar words and is easy to pronounce (and the second most spoken language in the world.)

Dutch and **Portuguese** are relatively easy, as is Indonesian. However, unlike most Asian languages, Indonesian uses the Latin alphabet. And unlike English, you pronounce it how it is spelled.

Italian is a language where you add an 'o' or an 'a' to the ends of English words and hope for the best. Italians are marvelous at sign language.

Now for the real challenges for English speakers:

Mandarin is the most widely spoken native language in the world. Their writing system is quite different from the

Latin alphabet, and the tonal quality of the speech affects the meaning of words. One example is the word 'ma.' It can mean horse, scold, rough, or mother, just according to what tone you use to say it.

Arabic is another language that is very hard to learn for English speakers. There are so many variants, so where do you start? There are 28 letters, but often the vowels are omitted, and they write from right to left.

So how will you choose which language to learn?

SUMMARY

South Koreans have enormous energy and enthusiasm for work and play.

Hiking in their incredible natural parks enables them to relax, find a sense of peace, and be one with nature, and the scenery is exciting and varied. Fencing is an activity you may not have thought of taking part in. Music seems to be common to all cultures as old as humankind. But if you want to give your brain a workout, try learning a foreign language.

Hiking
Folk Music
Fencing
Learning a Foreign Language

TURKEY

Turkey is unique. It lies in Asia and Europe, with a bridge and a barrier.

The land is mostly mountainous, with dramatic cliffs and high summits. Mount Ararat is 16,945 feet (5,165 meters) high. There are climatic contrasts between the high interior and the coastal areas, marked by summer droughts and harsh snowy winters.

Turkey is full of natural wonders and man-made historical buildings and architectural sites. For example, Istanbul has the stunning Byzantine Hagia Sophia Mosque. One of the world's most beautiful buildings and the largest church for over 1,000 years. And not far away is the sumptuous Topkapı Palace, the palace of the sultans and their harems.

Ephesus has a tremendous archeological interest, mighty Roman ruins, and roads with marble columns. Natural wonders include the rocky valleys of Cappadocia, together with the churches and homes cut into the rock.

But for hobbies, I have found ones that people enjoy when they are not working or sightseeing, and we will start with the cats.

CATS AND TURKS

When you visit Turkey, you will see many, many cats. It has been estimated that Istanbul has possibly over a million feral cats. You may find cats sitting on the bus, on the ferry, in the subway, in cafes, and on the street.

Why is this?

Turkey has a policy of not hurting or capturing these cats. They are seen as communal pets rather than unwanted strays.

When the Ottomans settled in Istanbul, most houses were made of wood and harbored rats and mice, so cats were valuable. Cats are also very clean animals. In addition, if you look at a cat's forehead, you can see above both eyes an "M" shape, said to be a sign that Muhammad blessed the cats, or so it is said by some.

But it does mean cats have a long and respected history in Turkey.

In Istanbul, there are vending machines for cats and dogs. People can put in a few coins as they pass by, and the money is used to feed cats and dogs. It seems a very humane way of dealing with these animals.

Even if you don't have a rat or mouse problem, a cat can be a wonderful pet if you are prepared to serve it and accept that your cat might be in charge. Having a cat can be a fun hobby, especially if you surround yourself with other cat owners, talking about all things cats.

BACKGAMMON

Backgammon is immensely popular in Turkey. Everyone seems to understand the game, which they call 'tavla.' If you visit Turkey, you will see backgammon boards out everywhere. Cafes, tea gardens, on the pavements, and every Turkish sailing boat, the gulet, will have one or more backgammon sets. And, of course, every household owns at least one set.

To play tavla well, you need skill and a measure of luck. The game is addictive as you learn the subtleties of playing well. Usually, this game is played extremely fast; the faster you play, the more skilled you are considered to be.

Although the game is vocal, Turkish people count the numbers where the dice rolls in their heads, not out loud. Backgammon is the world's oldest board game, originating in Mesopotamia thousands of years ago. As a result, many Turks know the numbers 1-6 in Farsi, which may be the only words they know in Persian.

You may find that backgammon is a very talkative game with players talking through their proposed moves and their consequences. It's a great way for strangers to meet up and play with an audience who also participates in verbal exchanges.

The game reflects the uncertainties in life – how will the dice roll? How best can you play on? So, why not set up a backgammon board and challenge your neighbor to a match, preferably with an audience and a nice cup of Turkish tea.

RUMMIKUB OR OKEY

Rummikub or Okey is a very popular game in Turkey. It originates in Germany, but Turkish expatriates and people living in Turkey enjoy playing Rummikub or Okey, which is similar.

Cafes and bars will often have a game of Okey running. The suggestion is that anyone over eight years can play, so it's an easy way for generations to mix in fun yet competitive ways. Usually, there are 2-4 players, but one can play online, with friends or family, or with people in far-off places around the world. It would be one way of keeping in touch when relatives have moved away. You can also pit yourself against computer opponents.

The game is a mixture of Mah-jong and rummy; it uses 104 tiles, which they call cubes, and draws many of the rules from rummy. So, it is easy to learn and involves grouping and ordering the cubes to make runs, just like the cards in rummy.

The cubes are numbered one to thirteen, and instead of suites, they are colored black, yellow, red, or blue, equivalent to two decks of cards. Each player starts with 14 tiles, and the player with the highest number starts the game.

Rummikub is said to benefit the brain because the hippocampus and prefrontal cortex, associated with memory and complex thought processes, are stimulated.

Okey or Rummikub is easy to play and makes a change from card or board games. If you want a sociable game with your friends or a solo computer challenge, then Rummikub might be a good choice.

OLIVE OIL SOAP MAKING

Soap is said to have been invented about 5,000 years ago in ancient Babylon. In Roman times, animal fats were used, but the Arabs and Persians produced the first soaps using vegetable oils in medieval times.

Olive oil soap has been made in Turkey since the 16th century. Because olive oil is abundant in the region, large soap-making enterprises evolved and now produce a wide range of enchanting soaps.

Turkish olive oil soap retains the natural ingredients, consisting of olive oil, salt – and natural scents like rose, thyme, lavender, and chamomile. In Istanbul or Izmir, the soap is presented naturally – large blocks on hay or straw; the blocks can be cut down to order. They are olive-green, white, or off-white. And the nice thing is that the olive oil soap is very inexpensive.

Fortunately, you can buy Turkish soap in many countries, and the natural feel and organic basis are becoming increasingly sought after. Olive oil soap is said to be good for the skin and strengthening the hair.

It is possible to make olive oil soap at home – and a bar of natural health-giving olive oil soap would make fine gifts and benefit yourself.

TEA & COFFEE – TURKISH STYLE

Tea

Turkey is one of the top 5 tea-growing countries globally, producing up to 10% of the total global production. And over half will be drunk by the Turks themselves.

The eastern Black Sea coast is full of tea farms; the mild climate, fertile soil, and plentiful rain make this an ideal growing area for tea. During the 5th century, tea was imported to Turkey via the Silk Road. Still, the boost to its popularity came when the Ottoman Empire fell after WWI, Turkey lost the coffee-producing areas, and coffee became very expensive. The country leader - Atatürk – encouraged tea drinking as a substitute.

Turks make tea in their own way. Two stacked kettles are used. The top is smaller, with the tea steeping in it for about 10 minutes, and the lower kettle has boiling water so that the tea drinker can dilute the tea to his or her taste. The tea is served in glass vessels, a cube of sugar is added, and the drinker holds the glass by its brim to avoid burning its fingertips. (Never add milk or lemon!)

Coffee

Turkish coffee is strong, though not as strong as espresso. When served in Turkey, they also serve a glass of water to clear your palette. While sipping the water, the fine coffee grounds will sink to the bottom of the cup.

The coffee is unfiltered so never stir it, or the 'mud' which sinks to the bottom of the glass will swirl around in the drink. The coffee is finely ground and often served with a small, sweet biscuit or sweet such as Turkish delight.

The coffee itself will often have sugar added to its preparation. Sometimes cardamon, a powerful antioxidant, will also be added to the coffee. You do not have to drink the silt at the bottom of the cup, but if you see someone turning the cup over after drinking, they may be telling their fortune from the pattern left by the dregs in the cup.

If you are lucky enough to have Turkish friends, they will probably be delighted to share their secrets of making tea or coffee the Turkish way. But if you do not know any Turkish people, you can still try your hand at making tea or coffee in perhaps a somewhat different way.

Invite your neighbor and get chatting over Turkish tea or coffee. It could be a great ice-breaker.

SUMMARY

Turkey has so much to offer, including incredible and varied scenery, archeology, and stunning buildings, but what do the people who live among such splendors do in their spare time? Turkey has many fun hobbies, from their love of cats to board games to making olive oil soaps. And finally, tea and coffee Turkish style. What better way to spend a few hours chatting with friends and family.

Cats and Turks
Backgammon
Rummikub or Okey
Olive Oil Soap Making
Tea and coffee Turkish style

OMAN

Oman is a small country with spectacular scenery, deserts, mountains, and the sea. The people of Oman have a long history and create beautiful crafts displayed in some of the best souks in the world.

The countryside is speckled with castles, forts, and tiny villages hidden in the mountains. There are isolated beaches, and the weather has hot sunshine for the sun worshippers, together with rains for the lush green countryside. Diving centers, water sports, and wild sea-life observation are hobbies enjoyed in Oman.

I have tried to find hobbies you can take on, in your own community. But nothing could beat the experience of a voyage into Oman, to meet the people firsthand, immerse yourself in a souk, and perhaps camp out under the stars under the clear desert skies.

WADI FUN – RIVERBED HIKING AND SWIMMING

Oman has a great variety of different terrains. Inland are craggy mountains, deserts, and wadis.

The wadis are dry riverbeds and make for exciting and interesting hikes. The possibility of flash floods no doubt adds to the excitement. So guides who understand the area and the weather not only add to the interest of the trip but also ensure the safety of the party.

The wadis can provide strenuous walking, so hiking boots are essential, as is carrying water. But the scenery is stunning! The wadi may be dry and arid but also feature natural springs and pools of water, reflecting the turquoise sky. Cooling off in the clear waters is an added charm.

Sloshing along a not-quite-dry wadi is a marvelous way to get the exercise we all need. In addition, wadis and rivers often have history embedded in their makeup. Water is where people have made their homes since the earliest of times. Every river, every stream has its stories to tell.

In Oman, away from the crowded cities of the coastal regions, you can find cliff-top villages where time seems to have stood still. You might discover irrigated terraces, date farms – and perhaps orchards of the rare frankincense tree.

Now, you may not have a wadi at your back door – but you may perhaps have a stream or a river? Following the bank of your local river can be an adventure of discovery.

There are plants, grasses, and trees. Do you know all of them? If you are lucky, there may be fauna to watch, water holes and fish in the water, frogs halfway between land and water, shy deer, badgers, otters, beavers, or foxes, and riverbanks are often teeming with birdlife both on and off the water.

In addition to the natural wonders of the riverbank, there may be history. The more you look into the past, the more fascinating it becomes. Who lived here? Have they left any traces? Are there documents to tell us a little about the people who made this place their home? In Oman, you can follow a Wadi, but you can explore a nearby stream or river back home.

SOUK MARKET EXPLORATION

If you like shopping, then you would love the Omani Souk. They seem to sell everything, much of it hand-crafted and often unique.

One of the oldest marketplaces in the world is the Souk of Muttrah, which can get very crowded. The colors, the scents, the calls of the merchants, and the vibrancy of life here, are so full of energy. It would be easy to spend a day just looking around.

You will find Omani pottery used for storing dates and grains, as water bottles, and frankincense burners simply for decoration. Palm leaf woven baskets and textiles in every color are just some things you can see on display.

How well have you explored your local market? Are there nearby ones you could compare it with? Market visits are an engaging hobby for many people, and they usually come home with something interesting to add to their collection.

SILVERSMITHING

Some of the loveliest crafts you can find in the souk is the silverware. Ancient jewelry is rare since when a woman dies, her jewelry is melted to form new pieces for her daughters. The original Omani silverware was made from Marie Theresa dollars (Thalers), the only source of silver in Oman. In Austria, these were minted in 1789, and Europeans brought them to Oman. This silver is smooth and silky to feel.

Silversmithing is a hobby that anyone can do – you don't need Thalers, and you can produce your own style of jewelry. You may need to attend classes to get started. But taken step by step, it is not too difficult. Sawing, then filing, are the first two steps. Then comes the forging, hammering, and making your piece into your desired shape.

It might be a good idea to practice on copper, which looks nice but is cheaper than silver. Soldering comes next, and then you can add the finishing touches, and voila – a unique item made by you. This might sound difficult, and maybe for some, it is. But this hobby is immensely rewarding for the individual who wants to learn this craft.

HALAWET AHMAD DESSERT MAKING

Omani foods are full of flavor. They use spices and colors and decorate their dishes with nuts and fruits, both savory and desserts.

Shuma 'The National Dish' is a roast using lamb, goat meat, or perhaps beef or camel. The meat is coated with a mix of spices, including cardamon, cumin, cloves, chili peppers, and coriander.

Many of their dishes are rice-based, such as chicken kabouli. A similar blend of spices livens up this dish, usually garnished with dates, chickpeas, sultanas, and nuts.

If you have a sweet tooth, you might like to try Halawet Ahmad, a traditional Omani dessert. To make it, combine roasted vermicelli (you can use colored vermicelli to make it more interesting) with condensed milk, desiccated coconut, butter, and almond powder. In Oman, the mixture is served as molded dome shapes and decorated with pistachios or almonds.

Here is one recipe for Halawet Ahmad:

Ingredients

1 cup butter
400 g vermicelli
1 tin sweetened condensed milk
1 cup almond powder
1 cup desiccated coconut

Method

- Sauté the vermicelli noodles in the butter until golden. Then add the condensed milk, almond powder, and coconut.
- Heat gently, stirring for 2 minutes. Let it cool a little, then transfer to molds.
- When it has cooled, it is ready to decorate and serve.

Once you have tried this out, it might become a popular, quick, and easy dessert to prepare. Making desserts might not be the healthiest hobby, but what if you turned it into a dessert club or for passive income by selling your desserts to a local restaurant?

BASKET WEAVING

Think of Oman, and you think of palm trees. They are everywhere. And Omanis don't just eat the dates; they also use palm leaves to make mukhraf and murbah - bags to collect the dates and intricately woven shoulder bags.

They also make baskets to store grain and dates or cook meat. Weaving palm fronds is an ancient Omani craft. They make furniture, mats, and coverings for food to protect it from insects.

The craft seemed to be dying out when four girls resurrected the palm leaf industry to produce a range of items, including luggage, storage boxes, dishes, and more.

Weaving is a hobby that has many variations depending on the type of material used, the colors, and patterns, the weave itself, and the range of finished products. For example, many hobbyists use willow bands to weave their baskets; others use textiles to make mats and rugs. In Oman, they use palm leaves.

If you are interested in trying it out, there are often classes you can attend, videos to watch, and DIY books to read. I bet that sitting in the sunshine weaving a beautiful basket is a very relaxing hobby.

SUMMARY

Oman has stunning scenery and many beautiful crafts. You can take inspiration from these, even though you may not have a Wadi in your backyard or a local market like a souk.

Weaving and silversmithing are both hobbies you can adapt to your own needs. Both can enable you to produce unique items which will give years of pleasure. Likewise, dessert-making can be very tasty and rewarding.

Wadi Fun - Riverbed Hiking and Swimming
Souk Market Explorations
Silversmithing
Halawet Ahmad Dessert
Basket Weaving

SCOTLAND

S cotland is a small country to the north of England and is part of the United Kingdom. Famously separated by the Roman Wall, named after Emperor Hadrian, the border areas have long been conflicted.

Scotland is mainly mountainous, with long sea lochs indenting the coast. The country is beautiful, sometimes remote, and wild. Dotted with fortified towers or peels and castles, you are never far from the history of this country. The Scottish people have held onto many traditional ways and the musical Scottish dialect.

One thinks of highland kilts and claymores, mists and mountains, lonely bothies, and sleepy fishing villages. Yet Scotland has contributed to explorers and adventurers all over the world, inventions we use every day, and culinary delights such as the haggis and the deep-fried mars bar.

I have picked out five hobbies you might enjoy but have a look at a recording of the highland games for a sense of Scotland today.

THE HOBBY

The hobby is a bird. It is about the size of a kestrel and visits Scotland between April to September. But it is rare and only restricts itself to a few sites. During the winter months, they live in Africa.

The hobby has a fine black 'mustache,' smart red 'trousers,' and long pointed wings like a large swift. The legs are yellow, as are their short chunky beaks. The feathers are black and tan, grey, orange, and white. So, they are smartly turned out.

This bird hunts on the wing and catches large insects, like dragonflies, small birds, like swallows, and bats. They often catch their prey with their sharp talons and transfer it to their beaks in flight.

They have been known to steal from other birds, such as kestrels. And their flight is a true aerobatic display. Very fast, very maneuverable, and very agile. Studying a rare bird allows one to become an expert, and the more you find out, the more engrossing they are. Beautiful masters of the air, what isn't there to like?

BURNS NIGHT

A Scottish Burns night is something to remember and treasure. Everyone dresses for the celebration. The women in long skirts, often tartan, a blouse, and maybe a tartan sash, held with a Clan brooch. But the men – ahh, the men – dressed in full glory in their tartan kilts, their dirks stuck in their socks, and their sporrans. The sporran takes the place of pockets and can be quite decorative.

Burns suppers are held all over Scotland and in many foreign countries. It's a celebration of the birthday of Scotland's national poet, Robert (Robbie) Burns. And there is a certain formality in the supper, but here is a typical example:

After the guests have taken their places, a procession takes place. Leading the procession is a piper playing the bagpipes as the haggis is piped in. The chief cook proudly bears the haggis on a large tray. This is laid reverently before the host. The host then exclaims the famous 'Address to the Haggis,' often ending it with a mighty blow from his sword to make the first cut in the haggis. Everyone toasts the haggis.

Then comes the meal. Haggis served with neeps and tatties. (Neeps can be turnip or swede, and tatties are potatoes – mashed.) It actually tastes good, especially with the natural Scottish accompaniment of real Scottish whiskey.

After dining, the main speech, the 'Immortal Memory,' is given. Then, there is a Toast to the Lassies and a Reply. Other entertainment may be provided by the guests who perform some of the bard's poems and songs. These can be delivered in quite a fearsome style.

To end the evening, the host gives a 'Toast of Thanks,' and then everyone stands up, links crossed arms, and sings Robby Burns' poem, 'Auld lang Syne.' (Note that the high road means the highway, but the low road means death.)

You can buy haggis for vegans and kosher haggis, but Americans cannot import the real haggis from Scotland.

There is nothing quite like a Burns night. It would take a lot of work to organize one, but it could be done, especially if friends join in the preparations. Of course, you would need a piper, a haggis, a few kilts, and a sword. But ending with Auld Lang Syne would make a Burns night a night to remember.

THE HIGHLAND FLING

The highland fling is a traditional dance of Scotland. It probably originated in the 17th century as a solo man's victory dance after a battle, usually against the English.

The dance is vigorous, precise, and athletic. Watching the dance helped the clan chiefs choose the most robust and disciplined men for battle.

Sometimes the precise movements are danced between the crossed blades of two swords. The 'fling' relates to how the dancer flings his (or her leg) behind or in front while hopping from one leg to the other. The dance is done with speed and lightness to the sound of the bagpipes.

The steps are intricate, and the order for the annual competitions may change. The dance is in 4/4 time, but the time has slowed from 192 beats per minute a hundred years ago to the present 114 bpm (which is still pretty fast!)

Watching the highland fling with the bagpipes wailing and the swirling kilts of the dancers is evocative of earlier times. You need to be fit to undertake this dance seriously, but there are videos to show you how if you fancy dressing up and trying it out. If the highland fling is too much for you, other Scottish dances are easier for the less fit.

GURNING

Gurning is an unusual sport and requires a strong sense of humor. It relates to pulling grotesque faces, traditionally through a horse harness.

In English, the word 'gurn' means "to snarl, to look savage," while in Scotland, the word means 'grin,' and the Irish use 'gurnin' to cry. Once a year, the gurning championship is held in Egremont, in northwest England, and close to the Scottish border, in their Crab Fair.

The rules are strict, no plastic teeth, no padding, or any other accessories. The winner is the man or woman who makes the most significant transformation of their face. Also, it makes for a great workout since you have 42 facial muscles.

You might try this north-of-England and Scottish hobby. We all pull faces from time to time, but who amongst your friends can pull the most distorted, terrifying face? Is it you?

HOME BEER BREWING

Scotland is renowned for its whiskey, with different areas having their own unique taste due to the water locally available. But distilling spirits is illegal in the UK, so many Scots have taken to brewing beer, and they find this a very satisfying hobby, as do their friends.

The start-up cost is not inconsiderable, and there is a steep learning curve, but once you have got into your beer brewing, it can become fascinating, and you are always learning new facts and experimenting to get the best results.

Beer-brewing is a very ancient hobby. Many home beer brewers start out using relatively cheap kits that are readily available. But there are some facts to consider before splashing out.

You need to ask yourself some questions before you start:

- Do you have room for the kit?
- Would you be devastated if your batch fails as they sometimes do?
- To begin with, it can be expensive, although it might save you money in the long run.

So why brew your own beer? It can be fun; you learn something all the time, a piece of history, a new recipe, etc. You make friends both in learning and in sampling the product. You can make your own unique tasting beer. There is a lot of help out there as the hobby of home beer making is becoming more and more popular. Sharing your experience on forums and reading other people's blogs is all out there, just waiting to be found.

SUMMARY

Scotland is a beautiful country with generous, strong, and inventive people.

The hobby is a bird, and as its name states, it must be part of this book. It illustrates the rare and robust colors and behavior suited to Scotland. Then we come to Burns Night. This is a part of a tradition in Scotland and is like no other ceremony.

If you want to keep fit, Scotland offers two somewhat different approaches, the highland fling, and gurning. Finally, after a hectic day gurning, why not settle down to your own home-brewed beer. You will have earned it.

The Hobby
Burns Night
Highland Fling
Gurning
Home Beer Brewing

CHILE

Chile is long and thin, with various climates, natural features, and traditions in different parts of this extraordinary country.

The name 'Chile' from the indigenous Aymara means 'Where the land ends.'

Chile has the driest desert in the world – the Atacama. Some places have had no rain since records began. When it does rain, fields of purple flowers stretch for miles. The highest volcano is in Chile at 22,615 feet and is active. The Chinchorro mummies are the oldest in the world, dating from around 5,050 BC. According to the Guinness Book of World Records, they also have their largest swimming pool.

Another record Chile holds is the largest earthquake ever recorded – 9.5 on the Richter Scale, which occurred in 1960 near Valdivia. It lasted a terrifying 11-13 minutes and killed over 1,000 people. In addition, Chile has roughly 3,000 volcanoes, about 36 of them active.

From this fascinating country, I have pulled out five hobbies you might like to try at home – one of them is not mummy making.

CHILEAN MUSIC

Music is enjoyed by over 60% of the population in Chile and is the number one hobby. Music existed in South America long before the Europeans came, and some aspects of this early music remain in Chilean Music. Then there is the Music of the Spanish conquistadors and modern music up to the present day.

Archaeologists have excavated many musical instruments from even the pre-Inca time. Complex musical systems with minor intervals, chromaticism, and scales with five, six, seven, or eight notes were in vogue, similar to other cultures in Asia and Europe.

In some areas of Chile, people still speak and sing songs in the ancient Cunza language. Later, music was to honor the gods, and modern music still retains elements of this culture. However, Christianity absorbed and added new favors, and now jazz and rock have been added to the musical mix.

You can buy local instruments such as the Trutruca (a kind of trumpet that incorporates a cattle horn to amplify the sound) or maybe a Pingkullwe (a transverse flute with five holes), a Huada (a rattle made from a pumpkin with small pebbles or seeds inside) and many other instruments.

The music varies just like the Chilean landscape changes from north to south. Still, now it has a national identity, and almost everyone loves to make music: rap or opera, orchestral or individual, there is something for everyone.

Folk music tended to be disregarded until governmental reforms in the 1960s and the New Chilean Songs movement emerged—this preserved Chilean traditions, from songs to recipes to proverbs. Then in 1973 came the military coup, and music suffered a significant setback like other forms of culture. But in the 1990s, the military regime ended, and music was reborn.

The variety of music in Chile is impressive. There are many instruments unfamiliar to other parts of the world. But whatever your taste in music is, as Kahlil Gibran wrote, "Music is the language of the spirit. It opens the secret of life bringing peace, abolishing strife."

What could be better than that?

FLAGS AND THEIR STORIES

The knowledge of flags can lead you to all sorts of historical facts, facts about battles, the way people thought when they drew up the flags, and the importance they might play in the lives of the citizens.

The Chilean flag has a horizontal divider, the top half white and the bottom half red. On the top corner of the hoist side is a blue square and a single white star in the square.

The colors come from the time when Chile was struggling for independence. White denotes the snow from the snowy peaks of the high Andes; blue represents the sky, and red, the bloodshed during the fight for independence. Added to these representations are the colors derived from the Chilean Indians – white for unity and freedom and the five points for the five provinces the country was originally divided into.

Every flag has a story to tell, whether it is the country's flag, more local, a festival or company, or a sport. Collecting images of them and discovering why they are as they are could provide you with hours of study, entertainment, and a lovely memento.

CHILEAN ICE CREAM (AND OTHER DESSERTS)

Chileans eat more ice cream than people in any other Latin American country, but they have some other fantastic desserts as well.

The desserts range from decadent cakes to cookie sandwiches to roasted milk. Let's look at some of them in more detail to whet your appetite.

Alfajores are the 'Chilean Oreos' – two round shortbread cookies sandwiching a spread, usually made from sugar and boiled milk. Coated with chocolate, desiccated coconut, or left plain, it's a treat.

Leche Asada or 'Roasted milk' – This decadent dessert is a rich mixture of eggs, sugar, and vanilla, in a flan case. The surface of Leche Asada is a crispy, toasted custard layer cooked separately in a hot water bath.

Leche Nevada or 'Floating Islands' – This popular dessert is egg-based; white, frothy meringue islands are floating on it. In Chile, the Leche Nevada is served in a small glass, and you eat it with a coffee spoon. This sweet dessert is straightforward to make and can be whipped up in less than ten minutes.

Torta de Mil Hojas or 'Cake of 1,000 leaves' – The leaves are thin puff pastry layers stacked high. Between them are manjar and walnuts. 'Manjar' is a sweet sauce, similar to caramel, with a smooth, rich flavor. Sometimes an acidic jam is added to counteract the richness of the manjar. This rich cake is often served at birthday parties or baptisms.

Cocadas – Simple and sweet, just eggs and desiccated coconut shaped into balls. If you need gluten-free desserts – then this is safe and simple.

Chilean Ice Cream – Chilean ice cream is exceptional. Here you can find flavors that are unique to Chile. Maybe the fruit used only grows in South America, such as eggfruit and custard apple. Carob is another popular flavor, and plants like Rica and chañar may flavor the ice cream.

You can easily make ice cream and find unique flavors that delight you. Sounds like a delicious hobby to take up.

POETRY COMPOSING

Chile is known as the 'country of poets.' Two Chilean poets have won Nobel prizes for literature.

Gabriela Mistral's passion was education and literature. She wanted to help others as she had experienced a childhood of poverty since her father abandoned his family when she was only three years old.

She empathized with the Indigenous Mapuche women who were badly treated, writing a sad poem ('Poems of the Saddest Mother') based on their experiences. She set up evening classes for the workers and gave voice to the women who, at the time, were not heard.

As a Nobel laureate, she worked at a girls' school when Pablo Neruda was a teenager, publishing poems and articles for the local paper, and she encouraged him.

Pablo Neruda became not only a renowned poet but also a diplomat and left-wing politician. He wrote his poems in green ink. To him, that symbolized hope and longing. He published his first book before he was twenty and the hugely successful 'Twenty Love Poems and a Song of Despair' soon after.

Chile has many other illustrious poets. The harsh landscape and political instability have provided a background for them, but maybe you have feelings inside you to express in poetry? The economy of words and the poem's rhythm make writing poetry a wonderful way to release your energy and maybe inspire others. Some of the

Chilean poets are worth reading to give you ideas for your own efforts.

UFO HUNTING

Do you believe in UFOs and Aliens?

As our explorations lead us deeper and deeper into space, we find worlds out there that might support life. So is it unrealistic to suggest that alien life has visited us?

If you want to see an Unidentified Flying Object (UFO), then Chile is the place to go. And, so far, we cannot explain everything we have seen in the night sky. The night sky of Chile is clear and dark. Pollution is minimal, and they have fine observatories in high places to peer through the atmosphere deep into space.

Many recorded sightings have occurred, including the 'Chilean Roswell' of 1998. Several witnesses thought a UFO crashed into a hill, and so convinced were they that special envoys from NASA and the Chilean army investigated and decided not to make their findings known.

Chile has an official UFO research bureau. It is part of the Air Force's duty to monitor unusual aircraft activity. "Watching the skies" is a popular Chilean hobby, with social media posts to back up their findings.

UFOs are often confused with airplanes, satellites, Chinese lanterns, and even meteorites. So how can you tell if it's a real UFO? Answer- you can't.

But you can study the phenomena and try to explain them scientifically.

It would be nice to think we are not alone in the universe. It is tempting to believe in UFOs but is that realistic or wishful thinking?

SUMMARY

We can't provide the volcanos or the clear skies, but the hobbies chosen can all be adapted to your own homes. Music is so varied in Chile that you can find almost any style to suit you. Collecting stories and images of flags can be strangely compelling, but if you need a break, the Chilean desserts will boost your energy levels, if only temporarily.

Poetry, like music, can be a very personal hobby. Finding the right words and rhythm can be daunting, yet writing poetry can be done anywhere. It's just a matter of finding a style that suits you. Finally, UFO spotting is a grand sport. After all, are we alone in the universe?

Chilean Music
Flags and their Stories
Chilean Ice Cream (and Other Desserts)
Poetry Composing
UFO Hunting

CROATIA

Croatia - a land with a thousand islands – is beautiful, friendly, and a place where people love sports of all kinds, including soccer, volleyball, basketball, handball, and water polo.

The country is predominantly Roman Catholic, so Catholic traditions and ceremonies are important in everyday life. Incredible medieval architecture survives in the City of Dubrovnik, which is very photogenic, with the Bokar fortress perched high above the Pile Gate, stern protection for the area. Dubrovnik is known as the 'Pearl of the Adriatic.'

I have picked out four hobbies inspired by Croatia that you might enjoy.

CHRISTMAS MARKETS

Zagreb, the capital of Croatia, has been named the top Christmas market in Europe for three years in a row. And it runs for about six weeks.

Browsing amongst the stalls, mulled wine in hand amidst the cheerful crowds, will take you back to childhood. With snowflakes falling lazily and carols singing, you get a sense of the magic and love that Christmas is supposed to be about.

As adults, we probably prefer the giving to the receiving of gifts? But we also know our bank and credit card statements lurk in the background. How much better if we can prepare a little each month so that we are ready when Christmas suddenly steals upon us unexpectedly, despite the calendar. Our presents only need wrapping, our cards only need signing, and the Christmas cake needs a last tot of rum.

If there are Christmas markets near where you live, everything you can possibly want is there for the buying. But, last-minute shopping can be expensive, and you might not find the perfect gift you are looking for. But you can always buy ahead, ready for next year.

Many people like presents that show thought and originality, so making your own gifts most likely will be appreciated; a home-knitted scarf is more valuable than the most expensive shop-bought one, and a piece of jewelry, carefully crafted by you, is a gift to treasure. And homemade cards can show off your skills and be designed especially for the recipient.

So, go to the markets for inspiration, buy what you can afford and love, but spend time making your own gifts during the year. Many hobbies in this book lend themselves to that.

PUPPETRY

In 1919, the first Croatian puppet play was performed, called the 'Clever Donkey.' Then, after WWII, Croatia created a network of professional puppet theaters. Glove puppets and rod puppets were added to the original marionettes. At first, traditional themes predominated, a retelling of well-known fairy tales, but then a more modern style was introduced. The puppets became more symbolic and less realistic to look at.

By the 1970s, puppets were seen as a form of visual poetry, music, and mime. Puppet festivals, teaching, and courses in the art of puppetry have emerged. The Department of Theater History keeps details of puppet drama, sketches, press clippings, photographs, and texts.

Making puppets can be as simple as tiny finger puppets (which could fit into homemade crackers) to the elaborate marionettes the professional puppet masters use. Once you start, it is easy to become engrossed in puppet making as a hobby.

WATER POLO OR SWIMMING

Some say that you are never too old to start playing water polo. The rules of the game can be adapted for older players or those with disabilities.

Yet water polo has been assessed as the most strenuous summer Olympic game, based on strength, endurance, speed, and agility. And Croatians are very good at it, gaining popularity amongst the younger generations.

While water polo is excellent for building self-esteem and socializing, you might find you enjoy a less strenuous activity like swimming which is great for all ages.

Swimming burns calories, improves circulation, lowers blood pressure, and reduces your risk of heart attacks. It uses all your muscle groups to get a good workout. It's also a low-impact sport, so swimming can be an excellent way to keep fit without the risk of injury or strain on joints. Why not check for pools in your area and find suitable times when they are not too crowded, so you can take your time and enjoy a good swim.

CROATIAN PALAČINKE CREPES

There are many kinds of pancakes and many types of crepes. Palačinke is a mixture of the two without needing a leavening agent. They originated in Roman times and have remained popular ever since. Cooking can be a rewarding hobby, especially when you become known for that one special food.

The batter is thicker than crepe batter but thinner than pancake batter – and the results are mouth-watering. It will keep for up to three days in the fridge. The crepes can be stuffed with savory or sweet fillings, prepared in advance, and even frozen between sheets of waxed or parchment paper.

Kept in an airtight container, you can take out as many as you want and reclose the container (although it will be tempting to remove them all.) Then pop them in a pan or the microwave for a tasty treat.

Street vendors sell them, families have their own special fillings, and they can be a meal in themselves. Moreover, they are quick to prepare; here is one well-tested recipe that makes about ten crepes:

Ingredients

3 large eggs
1 cup milk

1/2 cup club soda – this makes them light and airy
1 cup all-purpose flour
1/2 teaspoon fine salt
1 1/2 to 2 tablespoons butter, divided
1 1/2 to 2 tablespoons avocado or grapeseed oil

Method

- Whisk the eggs and milk together and mix in the club soda.
- Add the flour and salt and whisk to remove most of the lumps. This is the tricky bit – cover and let it rest for half an hour at room temperature.
- Cook in a skillet in thin layers, using a mix of oil and butter.
- Brown each side and turn it out onto a plate.
- Stack them until all are cooked – serve and enjoy.

PHOTOGRAPHY

Croatia has them all if you like stunning views, interesting snapshots of life, and ancient urban landscapes. You can find a vast library of beautiful photographs featuring Croatia, and it's worth trawling through some of these for a pleasant afternoon's occupation when it's raining outside, and the fire is cozy and warm.

Much of 'The Game of Thrones' was photographed in Croatia, making excellent entertainment for a winter evening if you like that kind of thing.

But anyone can take photographs. They not only provide a commentary on your life and interests, but they can also produce some artistic items to display. Better still, digital photography has many ways to correct mistakes, emphasize the good points, change the colors and proportions, and make a simple photograph a work of art.

All you need is a digital camera to start producing some fine images. Later more expensive equipment might be required, but photography offers an enormous range of opportunities. You can find many programs on the internet, from simple ones like Canva to more complex programs, so why not give it a go and create some fantastic photographs.

SUMMARY

Croatia is a land that welcomes you. The people are hospitable, and the place can give you a nostalgic sense of childhood. There is magic in the air.

Christmas Markets
Puppetry
Water Polo or Swimming
Croatian Palačinke Crepes
Photography

ICELAND

Iceland is beautiful, and despite a somewhat harsh climate, Icelanders have some of the longest lifespans in the world. But the population is small, around 320,000 people. Counting all the people who have lived here since the Vikings settled in the 9th century, the number comes to less than one million. But if you count the tourists who visited in just one year, the number approaches double that.

Iceland is a land of contrasts, hot thermal springs and glaciers, volcanoes and cold seas, and for some, a tongue-in-cheek belief in elves. They have some delightful customs – Husband's Day and Wife's day, Bun Day and Beer Day, and Sjómannadagur – a day devoted to the Seamen of Iceland. They also have a 'Party Weekend' or 'Merchant's Weekend' at the start of August.

Per capita, people believe Iceland has the most beautiful women in the world, the strongest men, the most Nobel

Prize winners, the best baseball team, and so on. In addition, Iceland is often top of the list for the most naturally beautiful country, the most LGBTQ friendly, the most gender-equal, and the cleanest country.

There are some seemingly odd customs, though. At various times, beer was banned, dogs were banned, and whistling or singing outside was banned.

Their hobbies reflect their Viking inheritance, so let's see what I've chosen.

GENEALOGY

There are only about 320,000 people who call Iceland home. They are nearly all descended from a small group of Vikings, but the interesting part is that the DNA shows that while the men are largely Viking, the women have the DNA of Celtic ancestors. What this means is open to interpretation, but did the Viking raiders seize the women from mainland Scotland and carry them off to their lair in Iceland?

Genealogy matters – you do not want to inadvertently engage with a close relative. Some students developed an app with the tagline, "Bump in the app before you bump in bed." There is also a highly popular website that offers access to Icelandic family trees.

Have you looked into your own ancestry? Church records, deaths, and wills can be fruitful sources of interest. Making your own family tree may lead you down some interesting pathways. My English friend, for example, told me how her ancestor was hanged in the market square, and yet she has now become the mayor of that same town.

Your children and grandchildren might find the stories you discover fascinating.

PATTERNS IN KNITTING

Icelandic knitted garments are highly valued for their high quality and intricate patterns.

The Icelandic wool has been cultivated over generations to stand up to the elements in a climate that can be cold and wet. The original settlers brought their sheep from Norway in the 9th century AD, and the breed has remained purebred and not mixed with other sheep.

The sheep's coats are well adapted to harsh weather conditions. The outer layer is long and coarse – known as 'tog.' This layer is tough and water-resistant. The inner layer is softer and keeps the sheep warm even if some water evades the tog layer and seeps down into the 'pel,' or inner layer.

When these two layers are incorporated into Icelandic knitted garments, the human inside keeps warm even in the snow and rain.

When humans knitted the clothes, the tog and pel were separated, but with the advent of industrial knitting machines, that is no longer possible. 'Lopi' is the name given to the dual wool of Iceland, and the resulting garments are wonderfully warm in cold, icy weather.

The sheep have a range of colors in their coats – black, white, various browns, or grey. Traditional knitting patterns using the natural colors are a feature of Icelandic knitting, and one is said to be able to tell which family knitted a particular sweater by the pattern. These patterns are handed down through the generations and are unique to the family concerned. And knitting is not just for women – men have been knitting for hundreds of years.

Infants were said to learn to knit as soon as they could crawl! And the results were an important economic export. So knitting was never just for granny.

You can find Icelandic patterns to try out yourself and buy the expensive-but worth-the-price Lopi Icelandic wools. Knitting and producing something special is a satisfying way to engage the hands while listening to music or watching television. Why not set up a group knitting club?

FERMENTED SHARK

If you are brave and like to taste exotic foods – why not try Hákarl or fermented shark?

Icelanders can trace this back to the Viking era; they feel it is one way to keep in touch with their ancestral past. In those far-off days, the people needed to find food to last out the long winters, and sharks were plentiful.

But there was a snag. Shark meat is poisonous. The shark's meat contains high levels of trimethylamine oxide and uric acid. This mixture helps stop the shark from freezing in the icy arctic waters but is lethal to humans.

So, the Vikings had to find a way to make sharks' meat safe to eat and long-lasting. This is how they did and still do it.

First, the shark is beheaded and gutted. Then it is put in a shallow hole dug in the sand and covered with gravel and sand. Next, the mound is pressed with large stones, squeezing the fluids out.

The shark is left to dry out for a few weeks and then cured by chopping it up into pieces and hung out to dry further. This can take a few months. The strips of shark meat develop a crust – which is removed before eating.

People say it smells like very strong cheese, but if you can get past the strong ammonia smell, the fish is edible. Some people think of this as a delicacy and are prepared to pay high prices.

Visitors to Iceland can join a local food tour and experience the Hákarl firsthand. So, here's the challenge, can you stomach Hákarl? Or can your friends stomach Hákarl? Not really a hobby, but what if you got into delicacies from around the world? Learning, studying, experiencing, and sharing these foods?

SAUCES IN ICELAND

Icelanders love their sauces. And what a variety they have.

You might think a hot dog should have ketchup, mustard, and onions? Well, in Iceland, they have a special hotdog mustard called Pylsusinnep, which differs from other mustards. They also add ketchup and 'remuladi' (remoulade). This sauce is based on mayonnaise and is rarely used except on hotdogs. It is said that Pylsusinnep will be used "every day from now until the sun swallows the Earth." It's that important for the Icelandic hotdog.

But many other sauces are used, especially béarnaise sauce, gravy, mushroom sauces, and brown sauces. In fact, any sauce you can think of is quite likely to be part of Icelandic cuisine. They have a unique sauce for fish, meat, pizza, chips, and anything else. There are sweet sauces too, like caramel, chocolate, licorice, and many more for fruits and desserts.

Perhaps you have not been a big fan of sauces, but maybe you are missing something? There are many recipe books devoted simply to sauces, so if you enjoy your hand in cooking, why not study sauces and try some out? Could you even get inspired to create your own secret sauce?

TINY HORSES

Horseback riding in Iceland is rather special. Over 1,000 years ago, the Vikings brought their shaggy little horses to Iceland, and their breed has remained genetically the same ever since.

Breeding with other stock made the very qualities that enabled the Icelandic horses to flourish in the harsh climate decline. Because of this, the Icelandic Althing (their Parliament) banned importing horses to Iceland in 928 AD. So, they have been protected for over 1,000 years!

The Icelandic sagas and legends tell of horses. In the 12th century, according to the 'Book of Settlements,' a certain man owned a horse named Skalm. He let Skalm choose where her settlement should be. When she stopped walking and lay down, that was where her settlement was founded.

Unlike most horses, who have three natural gaits (maybe four), Icelandic horses have five natural gaits. Walk, trot, and gallop are usual, but add to these the Tolt and the Flying pace. The Tolt is smooth and fast. One foot is always in contact with the ground. You can hold a glass of beer while riding and drink the full glass at the end of a Tolt. The Flying pace is fast. Both legs on one side of the horse touch the ground at the same time.

Every two years, the National Icelandic Horse Competition is held, and people come from all over the world, but like several other things, betting is banned in Iceland.

These horses are small, so the maximum weight limit for the riders is 110 kg (240 lbs).

Now you probably won't have access to an Icelandic horse, but maybe there are riding stables near you. Even if you have never ridden, horse riding is both stimulating and relaxing. Perhaps restarting childhood riding lessons might be nostalgic for you. Loving contact with animals is said to be one of the most beneficial things we can do. So why not look into the possibilities close to home?

SUMMARY

Iceland has so much to offer. With its unique customs and breathtaking scenery with active volcanoes, glaciers, and hot springs, the hobbies reflect the Viking inheritance in these tough, independent people.

Genealogy is central to their way of thinking about themselves and is even mirrored in the lovely knitting, using

ICELAND | 95

natural fibers from their hardy sheep and familial inherited patterns. One can't leave Iceland without tasting their foods, disgusting or highly sought after according to your sense of smell. Maybe that is why they have developed their sauces into a fine art.

The gorgeous little sturdy horses make riding seem a very attractive past-time, and the interaction between horse and man or woman can be deeply healing.

Genealogy
Patterns in Knitting
Fermented Shark
Sauces in Iceland
Tiny Horses

NEPAL

Nepal was a land of mystery until it opened up to explorers, trekkers, tourists, and serious mountaineers. Mount Everest is the highest mountain in the world, and Nepal shares its summit with Tibet (Tibetan Autonomous Region of China.)

But mountaineering is not a usual hobby for the Nepalese. Instead, it's a job that is well paid but dangerous. Since the first expedition to Mount Everest in the 1920s, at least 90 Sherpas, the high-altitude guides and porters, have lost their lives on the mountain.

Nepal is also home to the famous elite soldiers, the Gurkhas, with their signature knives, the Khukhris. But Nepal is a haven of peace and tolerance, with a strong religious presence and traditional cultures alongside the imported western cultures and strong ties with Tibet.

Hobbies are often associated with religion, such as the making and turning prayer wheels, musical instruments, and dance masks. Now they make many of these for the tourist trade. Silver jewelry, often inlaid with turquoise, metal statues, and bells, are just a few of the crafts undertaken in Nepal. They also make unique paper from the inner bark of the Lokta plant, which is exceptionally durable, tough, and resistant to insects and mildew.

Let's look at four hobbies you might be able to adapt for yourself.

PICNICS NEPAL STYLE

Picnics are one of the most popular activities in Nepal. Stunning scenery and company you like contribute to the occasion. But what is perhaps different is the way the Nepalese organize the picnic.

They are seen as social gatherings where each guest brings a contribution to the feast. One just hopes that not everyone brings a salad! Part of the pleasure is in the variety and perhaps unexpectedness of the offerings.

In Nepal, the typical type of picnic is on a table in someone's backyard, but it's outside, and hopefully, the sun will shine. Other times the family will take a drive or maybe meet up with friends, and Nepal has so many lovely places to visit.

There are even official picnics, a time for staff to bond. Simple sports, singing, and dancing may take place. For others, it's just a time to relax in good company, and eating and drinking are pleasurable activities.

I expect there are some pretty places near where you live? So, drive out into the country with family and friends to picnic. It is a great way to spend an afternoon (or a day), especially if you do not have to prepare all of the food yourself.

ACRYLIC FLUID MOUNTAIN ART

Nepal is a country of mountains, so it is no surprise to find their art reflects this.

Acrylic fluid art is a form of painting that uses acrylic paint that is more fluid than traditional acrylics. The color pigments are the same, but the effects can be lovely, and mountains make fantastic subjects. Might you like to try fluid art?

In Nepal, you don't have to go far to see incredible vistas, but there is no reason why you can't make up your own mountains, seas, forests, or even abstract color and texture artworks.

You can buy fluid art supplies or make your own from acrylic paints, acrylic mediums, and water. Canvas makes a good base, but a wooden board is even better for longer-lasting works. You will need to prepare the surface and seal the finished item to make it waterproof.

If you need inspiration, check out Nepalese flow art, which you can find in a video or on the internet. You may not be able to produce a masterpiece on your first efforts, but the technique is easy to learn and the results magnificent. You may decide to introduce silicone which disrupts the flow and makes for a marbling effect.

There are beginner sets enabling anyone to produce stunning pieces of artwork, and it's great fun. You might even start a group in your kitchen or yard.

FELTING

For many centuries, felting has been a traditional occupation in the remote villages of Nepal. The material created is tough and warm, ideal for rugs to insulate their homes from the extreme cold.

Maybe you have accidentally felted a lovely woolen sweater and then thrown it away? It's so easy to do. But felting, appropriately done, lends itself to many creative arts. You can make hats, rugs, toys, shawls, and useful or decorative things.

Felting is possibly one of the oldest arts in Nepal. Practical and using available resources. In Nepal, it's usually sheep's wool from their tough, hairy animals. But this is a craft you can do at home. Since tourism is one of Nepal's most important economic trades, many felt items are made specifically for the tourist industry.

What does felting do?

The woolen fibers are compressed and bonded together to create a dense fabric. This can be thick, thin, shaped, and long-lasting. Many mammalian fibers mat together when wet, so moisture, heat, and movement are used to make felt. This can be done by hand, but your washing machine can save time and energy.

You need to look up the instructions for making felt if interested. You might like to buy a starter kit at first, but as you get experienced, you will want to branch out, experimenting and producing some unique and versatile felts.

This hobby is not very expensive and is not very difficult until you advance to intricate designs and tiny details. If you need inspiration, look at images of the articles for sale in Nepal.

As Oscar Wilde said, "The mark of all good art is not that the thing done is done exactly or finely, for machinery may do as much, but that it is worked out with the head and the workman's heart."

SINGING BOWLS

Controversy surrounds the origin of the singing bowls. Did they originate in Tibet, or do they have a Nepalese origin?

Indeed, when Tibetan refugees fled to Nepal, some brought their singing bowls with them. As a result, whatever the origin, singing bowls can be found all over Nepal.

The bowls may be handmade, although now many are made by machine for the tourists. They can be plain or engraved, and the older bowls were usually made from a copper/tin mix, a kind of brass called 'bell metal.' Other trace metals can be added. The 'bell metal' is hard yet elastic enough to vibrate well when struck. When you rub a small wooden stick on their rim, they 'sing,' a soft, mellow sound said to have healing powers.

In Nepal, many healers use meditation and singing bowls, which create an aura like a shield to protect your body from the world's negative energy. Yet these bowls have been used for hundreds of years by Buddhas as alms bowls. But, perhaps as a marketing tool, the 'singing' bit wasn't added until the 1960s.

If you own one of these beautiful bowls, then you are fortunate. If not, technology has come up with apps you can try that have healing frequencies. Some have been devised to help you get to sleep, and some have been devised with specific frequencies to target areas of your body that may be troubling you.

Indeed, music can change our moods, and music therapy has been successfully used for people with autism and those suffering from Alzheimer's disease, dementia, and strokes. Maybe you could try meditation with some gentle music to enhance the experience. Try out several bowls or apps to find ones that resonate with you.

SUMMARY

Nepal has so much to offer, but I wanted to find hobbies that you could do yourself, and climbing Everest might not be practical for most of us. However, trekking adventures in Nepal might well be something you would like to do, but I saved that for when you visit the country.

I liked the idea of a picnic when everyone contributes the food, a friendly and entertaining social occasion. Acrylic fluid mountain art appears fun and not too difficult to get started.

Felting leads to many possibilities; maybe that old sweater could be felted and turned into adorable slippers? Finally, why not try the gentle sound of the singing bowls to relax you.

Picnic Nepal Style
Acrylic Fluid Mountain Art
Felting
Singing bowls

JAMAICA

W hat do you think of when you think about the Caribbean? Pirates, coffee, rum, and reggae, maybe? But there are some surprises as well.

Jamaica is home to some beautiful waterfalls, gorgeous beaches, and a rich history that is now a part of the landscape. There are over 1,600 churches in the 4,244 square miles of Jamaica, the densest church population anywhere, and the Christian religion is paramount, public prayers commonplace.

Electricity came here before it came to New York and Ian Fleming wrote his 14 James Bond books here. 'Dr. No' and 'Live and Let Die' were also filmed here. The world's fastest sprinter, Usain Bolt, comes from Jamaica, like many other world-class athletes.

I have chosen four hobbies to give you a taste of this remarkable island.

PIRATES AND THEIR HISTORY

Once upon a time, Port Royal was a 'pirate utopia.' Back in the early 1600s, Port Royal was one of the most dangerous cities in the world and acted as a base for some well-known pirates, including the legendary Welshman Henry Morgan. It was ideally situated for pouncing on merchant ships since the trade routes were very close by.

The legends about Morgan are numerous but include the facts that he raided Spanish settlements and shipping, becoming a wealthy plantation owner. In addition, it's said he dabbled in alchemy and found the secret to eternal life. Yet as he died, he gave his 'magic' compass to one 'Jack Sparrow!' And the character of Jack Sparrow may or may not be based on a real pirate, the best known of all the Caribbean pirates, the infamous Blackbeard.

But what can you do as a pirate hobby? Their history is confusing, and unraveling it might be quite fascinating. Who were they? Where did they hang out? Who paid them (the English government?)

Drawing maps, learning about the trade routes, and revisiting some of their hideouts could keep one busy for many happy hours. If you have grandchildren, why not make a booklet for them, all about real pirates?

GOLF

You might be surprised at this choice of hobby, but Jamaica has some rather unique golf courses.

Some are challenging, some more relaxing, but golf is a game that suits the sweeping landscapes of Jamaica. Taking in the shorelines and the mountains, with harmonious views and historical monuments, the courses are varied and suit any handicap.

Jamaica has been building up a reputation for golf over the past few years, with names like 'The White Witch Club' and 'The Half Moon Club.'

Golf is a popular game the world over, and it is one you can join at any age, enjoying time outside. Golf is also a chance for private conversations and bonding with friends. The competitive element need not get in the way of a good workout, fresh air, and that well-earned drink afterward.

JERK SAUCE AND ACKEE & SALTFISH

Jamaicans love spicy food, and jerk sauce is spicy! So they add it to everything like fish, chicken, or meat, giving a rather unique taste to sometimes a bland dish.

Fortunately, you do not have to make it from scratch since you can buy original jerk sauce anywhere and purchase different recipes according to your taste and the type of food. Fish and meat may require specific spices to liven them up.

Most countries have a 'national dish,' and Jamaica has 'Ackee and Saltfish.' Ackee is a fruit of the genus Blighia. Why named thus?

In 1793, Captain Bligh, of 'Mutiny on the Bounty' fame, transported ackee from Jamaica to Kew Gardens, England. Sometimes it is called the ackee apple, native to tropical West Africa. But you have to take care since unripe fruit can cause a vomiting sickness and even kill you. You must avoid the black seeds at all costs. Wait till the fruit opens naturally and the outer pods are red. But the yellow flesh is delicious.

The salt fish is just codfish that has been salted. Together with the jerk sauce, they make a tasty and spicy dish. In fact, National Geographic ranked it as the second-best national dish globally, directly under the United States hamburger.

So why not have a Caribbean evening, add some reggae music, buy some jerk sauce and prepare Ackee and Saltfish for your guests. You are almost sure to want to repeat the experience.

REGGAE

Jamaican music includes mento, dancehall, rocksteady, dub music, and ska, but the most well-known is reggae. Reggae is based on ska and early Jamaican music featuring drums, bass guitar, electric guitar, and a scraper. The scraper is a corrugated stick that you rub with a plain stick to make a unique scraping sound. The heavy four-beat rhythm is characteristic.

Then came Bob Marley, and a legend was born. With his backing band, The Wailers, he hit the international scene with such songs as "Little Birds," "One Love," and "Redemption Song."

Reggae has become associated with the voice of the oppressed and is closely related to the Rastafarian movement. The songs are a powerful voice for empowerment.

Worldwide, people can empathize with the emotions and traditions associated with reggae. It's also a way of expressing political views – and maybe appears more truthful than some politicians' speeches.

Following the words and moving to the rhythm can be quite moving as the music speaks to our inner spirit, and reggae is no exception. Tuning into reggae can bring a taste of the Caribbean into your living room, and hearing the words can be thought-provoking. Luckily there is plenty about, such as CDs, the internet, and live concerts.

SUMMARY

Jamaica has a relaxed and pleasant land, great food, top athletes, and sometimes turbulent history.

Pirates are indelibly linked to the Caribbean, but golf seems surprising. You will love jerk sauce and ackee & saltfish, the national dish if you like spicy food. Music is a part of life here, and reggae is now a global voice for the disadvantaged and pleasant to listen to.

Pirates
Golf
Jerk Sauce and Ackee & Saltfish
Reggae

ESTONIA

E stonia has a combination of medieval history together with the most modern technology. It is a land with over 1,500 islands, lakes, and forests with a landscape sprinkled with hilltop fortresses and castles.

Tallinn, the capital, has a well-preserved medieval center, and although you can find many churches, Estonia is one of the least religious countries.

Estonia regained independence from Russia in 1991, and she joined the European Union in 2004.

Family life and oral traditions are key features in the life of Estonians; they look after their elderly. Cultural activities are popular, and nightlife and lazing on the white sandy beaches contrast with hiking and skiing. Estonia is a land of contrasts, medieval and modern, traditional and forward-looking. Here are some of the hobbies practiced in Estonia.

SINGING

"Without singing, there would be no Estonia."

Peeter Perens, conductor and artistic director of the 2019 Song Festival, said these words.

For many years, Estonia's beautiful language was the language of the peasants, but in 1869, Johann Voldemar Jannsen organized the first Song Festival. A feeling of nationalism arose – "We can be a Nation."

Songs were one activity where Estonians could feel like Estonians, although during the Russian occupation, these songs were forbidden. Large groups came together under the guise of singing, defying Moscow in singing for independence.

In June 1988, 100,000 Estonians gathered for five nights to sing protest songs until daybreak. There was a feeling of their language, their nation, their song. "The Singing Revolution" (1986-1991) culminated in 1988 when a huge song festival attended by 300,000 Estonians in Tallin, 40% of the population, made their desire for independence very clear. The Estonian flag was raised, Russian tanks were faced down, and Gorbachev gave them independence.

The songs in Estonia have two origins, the ancient Finno-Ugric culture and the German-Swiss culture. And everybody likes to sing.

Song festivals and choirs are especially popular in Estonia, and they have not only hosted it but they have also won the Eurovision song contest.

You can sing anywhere: in the shower, on the balcony, or join a choir and sing along with other like-minded people. Songs may celebrate new events or tell tales from long ago. Awakening a sense of belonging, stone age mothers probably sang to their babies, just as fathers croon to their young ones.

Singing is one of the best ways to relax the muscles of your face, where we often hold tension. So, open your mouth and let the music flow.

MEDIEVAL TOWNS

You may feel you have stepped back in time when you visit Estonia. The capital city, Tallinn, can trace its origins back to 1154. The 'Toompea,' the hill in the center, has medieval houses and winding cobbled streets. You can see the outlines of the old city wall surrounding the central area and explore the guard towers that remain today.

The old town was built in the 15-17th centuries, and exploring it on foot is a great way to enjoy the old town. If you get weary, there are green parks where you can relax. Students' cultural tours will include stories about the history of Tallinn through the ages. (And the tours are free.)

Tallinn also has an abundance of cafes where you can watch the world go by, a zoo, modern shops, a beautiful 19th-century Russian Orthodox church, and a cathedral that dates back as far as 1229.

You may not have such an ancient city to explore close to you, but everywhere has a history. Some places employ knowledgeable guides and oversee tours in places of local interest. Often these are people who have retired and have the time to learn about and then talk about the places. Maybe you would like to do this, or perhaps just root around yourself?

MUSEUM VISITS

Visiting museums is a well-liked pastime in Estonia. In 2018 there were 3.4 million visits, averaging about 2 per person. However, this is still less than the previous year.

Museums of art were the most visited, especially the Estonian Art Museum. The Kumu Art Museum is the main Art Museum. The central part is based in an attractive modern building and displays Soviet pop art and contemporary art and provides an overview of Estonian art.

The Kadriorg Art Museum is based in a baroque castle built for the Russian Tsar Peter and shows early Russian and European art. Educational programs and exhibitions help to interpret the old masters. There are also over 250 sculptures created in the 18th – 20th century for people to admire.

Visiting museums can open our eyes to other cultures, to artifacts from previous ages, and when we take our time, a visit can lead to several follow-up research projects. It's odd how we often do not visit places on our doorstep. Museum visiting can be an interesting hobby, and you might even like to become involved in volunteering to show people around, as museums are often short of staff.

CROSS-COUNTRY SKIING

Estonia has some excellent cross-country skiing areas where you glide through beautiful countryside as you tone up your whole body under safe conditions.

Before taking up any sport, you should consult your physician, but cross-country skiing is not as potentially arduous as downhill or ski jumps.

Empty forests, snow gilding the trees, flattish plains for easy skiing, and well-organized ski trails make Estonia a haven for cross-country skiing. (And if you are fortunate, you might also see the northern lights since Estonia is one of the best places to observe them.)

Skiing can be kinder to your body than running but gives a superb workout. Every muscle seems to be used, circulation improves, and cheeks glow. You can escape the crowds or ski with friends. No noise except the swish of your skis, your breathing, and perhaps the laughter of your companions.

If you are a beginner, it is a good idea to tone up your body first since cross-country skiing will be demanding. If you have weak knees, you must ask your doctor first.

Beginners need flat places to start and only then gentle hills. Soon, you will be able to undertake longer journeys in lovely scenery, and when you fall, the snow will soften the bump.

Exercise releases endorphins or 'happy hormones,' so you will feel fantastic.

THE INTERNET

Estonia is possibly the most advanced country in the world regarding using the internet and similar technologies. Does this surprise you?

This is awesome. Not long ago, Estonia was a poor backwater under Russian domination. But now they have an impressive set of technological achievements.

They have E-residency, E-government, mobile parking, and fully online banking.

Most money transactions can be done online, and the population is well educated in digital technology. Children aged six are taught, and the seniors have also been included since pensions are only paid electronically. Estonia aimed to become a 'digital nation.' In 1996, they had online banking, and mobile banking started in 2000. Electronic signatures and e-signatures began in 2002, and smartphones in 2010. So, you may never need to visit your bank or use cheques or cash.

Everywhere there is free wifi, and you can complete your tax returns online with great ease. They have ID cards and digital signatures. Estonians created the first skype software.

Your computer can be your best friend if you have some knowledge of using it. It is a wonderful source of information on every subject you can think of, but there are times when most of us could happily sling it out the window!

Maybe a hobby that would appeal to you would be to learn more about computer use? There is coding design and so much more.

SUMMARY

Go back in time or become extra modern and computer savvy. Estonia offers it all. I chose singing as our first hobby since it has been very important in gaining independence for Estonia.

Going back in time in the medieval city of Tallinn offers opportunities, and visiting museums adds to the experience. Cross-country skiing is mentally and physically challenging but remember to ask your doctor.

Singing
Medieval Towns
Museum Visits
Cross-Country Skiing
The Internet

~

I hope that the wheels are turning and you are thinking of ways to enjoy life to its fullest by starting new creative hobbies. I wrote this book for people just like you and me, transitioning into retirement or already into your golden years.

As a Health & Life Coach, it is important not to leave anyone out. Everyone deserves to live a vibrant life, so if this book has brought you some joy, a glimmer of hope, or a solid plan to improve upon your day-to-day, I have a favor to ask you. Please stop what you are doing right now, and go to your computer or phone and leave a review wherever you purchased this book.

Your review will greatly help other readers decide if this book is for them. Thank you for taking the time to leave a review.

SOUTH AFRICA

S outh Africa is a land with much to offer. The precious Kruger National Park, with wild animals, forests and beaches, cliffs, and the famous Table Mountain overlooking the Cape of Good Hope at the southern tip of the continent of Africa.

South Africa became independent from Great Britain in 1910. Many years of apartheid followed, but now the legal system gives similar rights to all.

However, the rich and the poor might have very different hobbies - yachting and sailing, collecting fine wines, or art, are popular with the rich, whereas arts & crafts, gardening, knitting/crocheting, and baking are pastimes for others.

Sports like Nguni stick-fighting and Dambe boxing are popular, especially Capoeira, a mixture of martial arts and dance originated in Angola. However, I have picked out common hobbies you can enjoy at home and those South African people enjoy.

ONLINE COURSES

One of the most significant increases in interest in South Africa is online courses. Almost twice as many people are interested now than just a couple of years ago.

Some courses that South Africans seem to target are higher education certificates in tourism, digital marketing, and paralegal studies. They are also interested in SEO, computer courses, and sales management, among others.

As technology improves, so do the learning opportunities, and many fascinating courses are on offer. Three that took my eye were "Extinctions: Past and Present," "Understanding Clinical Research: Behind the Statistics," and "What is a mind?" all available in South Africa.

Maybe the best course to start with would be something about project management to keep your studies on track?

Online courses offer an almost endless supply of study opportunities, whether you want a certificate at the end or simply to learn about new subjects. The people of South Africa are taking advantage of these. Are you?

CROSSWORD CREATION

Crosswords have become increasingly popular in South Africa, as well as in many other countries. In fact, in South Africa, internet searches for crosswords have increased by 88% since the pandemic that started in 2020.

South Africa has its own unique vocabulary since several languages might be spoken there, and some of these words can end up in South African crosswords. Words like:

Lekker – nice/great – we had a lekker party
Howzit? – who is it?
Yebo: yes – comes from the Zulu
Shap sharp – all's fine
Braai – BBQ
Yoh – surprise
Robot – traffic lights

Maybe you are good with words? Possibly a challenging brain workout for you? Perhaps you could make your own crosswords, especially on a subject you know something about?

To make it easier, here are a few tips:

Choose a theme and then write a long list of words about it, short and long words. Try to link some of the longer words together. This will be the center of your grid. Fit shorter words around them.

Build up your grid with blank squares, number the first letter of every word, and create the clues!

Crosswords are in demand. Newspapers feature them, books about them are on sale, and it is possible to make money by creating and selling them.

JUKSKEI

Jukskei is a sport unique to South Africa, although it is gaining popularity across the continent.

Jukskei originates from the Afrikaners' name for the wooden pin used to yoke oxen. Around 1743, transport riders traveled by wagons drawn by oxen. They used to throw the pins at a stick planted in the ground, attempting to knock it down. The game has formal rules and is supervised by the International Jukskei Federation.

Usually, this game is played with teams of two or four, and the distance to the stick is fixed. In 2017 by the South African government, Jukskei was included in the Indigenous Games Project.

One of the largest rivers in South Africa is also named the Jukskei River, which is a branch of the Crocodile River.

This game, or your interpretation, could be quite competitive, easy to set up, and suitable for a laugh. Just keep any dogs well clear unless they could be used to retrieve your 'pins.'

MALVA PUDDING

South African food is as diverse as its different peoples. Dutch, German, English, and French mix with the many local tribes, and their unique blends of culture and cuisine have evolved into very tasty dishes.

Meat is an important ingredient in many of the foods on offer, but the desserts are to die for! Here is one sweet treat you might like to try. The origin is Cape Dutch, and it's called Malva Pudding.

Ingredients for the pudding

6 ½ ounces sugar
2 large eggs
1 tablespoon apricot jam
5 ounces all-purpose flour
1 teaspoon baking soda

½ teaspoon salt
1 generous tablespoon butter
1 teaspoon vinegar
⅓ cup milk

Ingredients for the sauce

¾ cup fresh cream
3 ½ ounces butter
3 - 5 ounces sugar
⅓ cup hot water
2 teaspoons vanilla essence

Method

- Preheat oven to 180°C (350°F). Grease a baking dish 18 x 18 x 4 ½ cm (7 x 7 x 1 1/2 inches).
- Whip the sugar and eggs until thick. Then add the jam and mix.
- Add the melted butter and vinegar.
- Pour into the greased dish and bake until brown and risen – about 30-45 minutes (You may want to adjust the heat and time according to your oven.)
- To make the sauce, melt all the ingredients together, stirring well, and be ready to pour it over the pudding as soon as it comes out of the oven.

The hard part is leaving it to stand for a while before serving to allow the sauce to seep through.

In South Africa, they often serve this with ice cream or cream. As a winter treat, this pudding will warm the cockles of your heart. Baking can be a gratifying hobby, and I think your family and friends will agree.

CROCHETING

During the Irish potato famine, crochet came into being. It provided an income that was desperately needed.

Crochet is satisfying and quick. It's faster than knitting once you know how to do it. And it is so satisfying to create something you made yourself. In South Africa, crocheting has also provided an income for some of the poorest women, who may not have time for more demanding hobbies.

Workshops have sprung up where people can meet up, socialize, and enjoy crafting a practical, durable, and attractive item.

There are only five basic stitches, with many ways to use them, from simple squares to make shawls and blankets to delicate filigree shawls and Christening robes. This hobby is easily carried from one place to another and can be done while watching television or the children.

As a new starter, many YouTube videos can take you through the stitches step by step and show you how to read patterns. Just be sure you know whether you use European or American names for the stitches since there are differences.

If you are interested in selling your items, why not showcase them on Facebook, Etsy, or Pinterest?

SUMMARY

South Africans enjoy various unusual games and hobbies, like Nguni stick wrestling or cheetah walking, which would not be easy for us to copy. Still, they also have some very familiar things we can do at home.

More and more variety in online courses and the ease of access make these a viable proposition for most of us. Crossword creation is another way to stimulate the brain. If you want something more active, try your own version of Jukskei or to relax, settle down to create something practical with your crochet hook.

Online Courses
Crossword Creation
Jukskei
Crocheting

SAMOA

F a'a Samoa means the Samoan Way. This has meaning to Samoans and influences the everyday lives of the Samoan people. Fa'amatai is a social system where family and village elders are expected to put the community's interests above their own interests.

This in-built service to others continues to this day, and if you visit Samoa, you will be welcomed with warm smiles, hospitality, and respect. In Samoa, the elderly are respected, and their opinions are sought. Their long experience in life is valued. Likewise, children are brought up to pay attention to their elders and obey their parents until they marry.

Many of the activities undertaken by the Samoan people are geared toward family and community bonding. Outdoor activities like surfing, diving, sea-kayaking, and island excursions are popular. They also enjoy uma cuisine, traditional crafts, cake decoration, and a DIY form of cricket called kilikiti. And for a day out, there is always the Robert Louis Stevenson Museum to visit since he used to live and write in Samoa.

SAMOAN UMU COOKING

In a typical Samoan village, the umu is a common way of cooking, and very little is needed in terms of equipment. This is not fast food, but one umu can feed many hungry people. It is an integral part of the Samoan way of life.

The umu is an oven made above the ground but uses hot volcanic stones to provide heat. Traditionally the earth oven is placed on a 'fale,' a unique stand for the umu.

Typically, the umu cooking method is handled by men, just as BBQ often is in western cultures. But anyone can use the umu cooking method.

The volcanic stones are heated up in a fire. All this takes time, so the cook might have to get up early. Volcanic rocks are good because they retain heat well. The fire is ready when the wood and coconut husks are burnt to cinders.

You first must prepare the food to load into the umu. Food may contain meat, fish, or octopus, often combined with coconut cream. Vegetables and fruit such as taro, ulu (breadfruit), and unripe bananas may be added, plus the favorite, palusami (coconut milk) with onions.

The food might be wrapped in coconut fronds, banana leaves, or coconut halves. Then the food is placed on top of the hot stones, with some stones placed gently on top. More banana leaves are settled on top to seal in the heat, so you have to wait!

Usually, the food takes around 90 minutes to bake, giving off a tantalizing, smokey yet savory, and sweet smell with a hint of coconut. Samoans have been smelling this aroma for over 300 years. The umu can be used for large families or small gatherings and is an easy way to cater to a larger group of people.

The Samoan umu is like the western BBQ, with its distinctive flavors and foods. You might try a version of the umu in your own backyard.

'IE TŌGA

The Samoan embroidered mat isn't a mat at all, even though we call them 'fine mats' in English. Made roughly the size of a bed cover, they are far too valuable to tread on.

Myths surround the origin of these fine mats. One story tells the tale of the goddess Nāfanua. She planted the first pandanus from which these mats are made at Falealupo. Near the entrance to Pulotu – the Samoan equivalent of Hades – this lies in the sea where the setting sun lights up a golden pathway.

The pandanus has a fan of long, narrow leaves and aerial, woody roots. There are two sub-species of pandanus used for mat making, the very fine one and the other a little coarser. Both types of pandanus are now grown in the villages: the more delicate the weave, the more valuable the mat.

In the past, the 'ie tōga was used as currency, but now it is used in special occasions such as processions, funerals, weddings, and the blessing of a new house or church. 'Ie tōga might be worn on special occasions, like the lavalava tied around the waist. The women make these mats, often as a communal activity, and some of the finest mats can take months to finish. The resulting shine and softness add to the value.

But what makes these 'ie tōgas so special?

Not only are they finely woven, but they are also embroidered with images and designs in colored threads and materials. They sport a fringe and a strip of red feathers (now often dyed chicken feathers.) They make valuable gifts and may be passed down to the family as heirlooms. In the past, they represented family wealth.

Now you may not have pandanus growing in your yard – and you might not want to spend months making a bedspread-sized 'mat,' but the idea of an embroidered mat is versatile.

One suggestion is to weave a mat from linen strips and then embroider it in any way you wish, appliqué and colored yarns could make your mat unique, and a small mat would make an interesting table mat for special occasions or be given away as gifts. You could even match it with table-napkin embroidered rings.

You could find plenty of images of Samoan 'ie tōgas for inspiration on the internet.

SAMOAN CAKE DECORATING

Samoa cake decorating is an art. You can see some truly unique creations from Samoa on Pinterest. Samoans thrive in cake decorating, and skills are often passed down between generations.

One example I saw was the 'Grandpa Cake.' It costs $355.00 or 6 weekly interest-free payments of $59.16, but it has a five-star rating and several flavor options. It looks far too good to eat!

There are options for cake decorating courses run in Samoa or online. You might never achieve the star quality you can see on the cakes created in Samoa, but it is an exciting hobby for the creative person.

Most everyone likes some sort of cake, and the nicer looking it is, the better. Birthdays, Christmas, and other festive days often have cake at the heart of the celebration. But not everyone has the time or the talent to create beautiful cakes. If this is something you aspire to, online or in-person instruction would be very helpful. The best thing about this hobby is that your mistakes can be eaten, and no one needs to know.

KILIKITI

English missionaries brought the game of cricket to Samoa in the early 19th century. The game is now the national sport of Samoa, but with Samoan alterations. And kilikiti is widespread around the Pacific Ocean (but not in England.)

Players in this form of cricket wear no protective shields or padding. Their traditional lavalava sufficed. This is a wrap-around skirt made from a single piece of cloth. But the ball is very hard. It is made from a hard rubber wrapped in processed pandanus leaves.

The bat is modeled on the three-sided traditional Samoan war club. It is made from wood and wrapped in sennit. Each player can have his bat, differing in length and surface angle, so it can be almost impossible to work out where the ball will be headed.

Just as bats are unique, so to are the rules flexible. In fact, only the players may know what the rules are for any given game.

However, there are some ways in which kilikiti resembles English cricket. They have fielding and batting teams and a pitch. They alternate bowlers from one end of the pitch to the other, with two wickets. The teams can be any size, and visitors are often welcomed in.

Kilikiti is very much a communal event. Everyone takes part or watches, and the kilikiti matches are fought as enthusiastically as any English cricket game.

Because you can make up your own rules, you might try a game of kilikiti in your backyard, but you don't have to field a very hard ball; just have some fun and light exercise.

SUMMARY

Samoan people are warm and friendly, and their code of conduct ensures that other people are cared for and respected. Their hobbies reflect this. Umu cooking is a slow process that gives ample time to chat and socialize with family, friends, and visitors. While you wait, you could always make a woven mat and decorate it. Cake decorating is brought to new artistic highs and kilikiti, which is just fun with few rules, or make them up to suit your team as you go along.

Samoan Umu cooking
'Ie Tōga (Fine Mats)
Samoan Cake decorating
Kilikiti (Samoan cricket)

LIECHTENSTEIN

The Principality of Liechtenstein is a tiny country between Switzerland and Austria. It is a financial center, previously a tax haven.

The head of state is the heir designated to the throne, Prince Alois. Just over 70% of the people are Catholics, so religious celebrations, as well as Valentine's Day and Mother's and Father's Days, are kept.

The main crafts used to be barrel making, basket weaving, and clog carving, although now sculpture, pottery, and woodcarving have taken over to a large extent. Liechtenstein is the world's leading exporter of false teeth.

Liechtenstein might be a small country, but it has some interesting hobbies.

CLOG CARVING

Carving clogs is a traditional hobby in Liechtenstein; although many of the clogs are made in Holland, then a hand-carved design is added in Liechtenstein.

Clogs are comfortable to wear, easy to slip on and off, and can make interesting decorations.

In Liechtenstein, doorways, and entrances often feature wood carvings. They may be flowers or a row of hand-carved clogs, sometimes with natural (not carved) flowers growing within them—what a change from ordinary flowerpots.

A set of stamps celebrates traditional crafts in Liechtenstein and feature a wagon wheel, a milk pail, and a clog.

Suppose you would like to carve something unique and not too tricky; videos on the internet explain how to go about it. First, you need to buy the plain clogs and then simply decorate them by coloring and varnishing them and then hanging them up or wearing them. After that, they are sure to be admired.

RIBEL

Ribel (or Rebl) used to be a poor man's dish in Liechtenstein. Healthy and filling, its base is cornmeal, so it's gluten-free. Now many restaurants offer Ribel, often for breakfast.

Cornmeal is a coarse flour made from maize, and maize cultivation in this area has been ongoing since at least the 16th century. Many families planted maize in their gardens. It made a perfect breakfast before a day of hard labor in the fields and was a great stand-by during the turmoil of the world wars.

To make Ribel, cook the corn, possibly with wheat, in boiling water or milk, then roast it with butter. Add apple puree for extra taste.

Here is a recipe for you to try out:

Ingredients

300 ml milk
300 ml water
1 tbsp salt
500 g Ribel corn/semolina corn
1 tbsp grapeseed oil
25 g butter

Method

- Boil the water and milk with the salt.
- Stir in the corn, and simmer over low heat. If you continuously stir it, you are less likely to create lumps. It thickens to a paste which you cover and leave for about 3 hours.
- Heat the oil in a frying pan, add the Ribel mix, and roast in the pan for about 20 minutes. Stir

often and add the butter bit by bit. It will turn a golden brown.

• Enjoy with a fruit compote and coffee.

Incidentally, you don't have to get up several hours before breakfast since the mixture will keep in an airtight container in the fridge overnight.

STAMP COLLECTING

Maybe you are a stamp collector? Liechtenstein has some of the most beautiful stamps in Europe, and it is possible to find them and build up a worthwhile collection.

For Liechtenstein, they are a source of revenue for the government since the stamps can be quite valuable. Often the designs are taken from the paintings in the art collection of the Prince. Otherwise, they might depict traditional occupations, such as basket weaving and barrel making.

The stamps of Liechtenstein are associated with the stamps from Austria and Switzerland. Before 1918, Liechtenstein was part of Austria. Separate stamps for the Principality of Liechtenstein only began in 1912.

Then Switzerland took over when the Austro-Hungarian Empire collapsed after World War One. It can be expensive to collect earlier stamps, but it might be possible to build up a complete collection if one starts with stamps from 1945 onwards.

Internet auctions are one source of stamps, but you could choose another country to specialize in or simply collect pretty stamps because they look attractive. Philately, the collection and study of postage stamps, has many possibilities.

MACRO PHOTOGRAPHY

This is a slightly different slant from the popular hobby of photography. It means taking extremely close-up photos, usually of small things, insects are a common theme, and making the photograph greater than life-size. It opens up a fascinating world you could not see with the naked eye.

This differs from micro photography, where the super-close up is reproduced life-size.

Liechtenstein has photo courses to help beginners capture stunning images. There are also internet and video courses and guides available. But this is not always the easiest of hobbies to become an expert at.

You will need the right equipment, for example, a tripod and the macro-lens, and you will need to be extra careful about the lighting and focusing. However, once you have your image, you can have fun cropping it, altering brightness, sharpness, and even color.

You can find the most amazing things to photograph in your own backyard, like details of flowers, an insect's eye, or the weave of the fabric you are wearing. There is no end to possibilities. You might wish to visit a museum where such photographs might be on display, such as the Smithsonian Museum of Natural History.

SUMMARY

Liechtenstein has a mix of new and old. The recipe for Rigel is based on a nourishing peasant breakfast, but macro photography is up to date. Wood carving has always been a feature of life in Liechtenstein, and collecting stamps is a global interest, with stamps of Liechtenstein highly coveted.

Clog carving
Ribel
Stamp collecting
Macro photography

EGYPT

Egyptian history goes back a long way. The old forms of entertainment included such things as javelin throwing, swimming, chariot racing, wrestling, juggling, music, and dance. Literature was also important. Ancient Egyptians wrote poetry, puns, and spells, and in modern times Egypt has produced some of the best Arabic writers.

Many ancient ways have continued; for example, senet is still played. Music and dance continue to be important; reading, crafts, and learning about the past are enjoyable activities.

AMATEUR ARCHAEOLOGY

Amateur archaeology in Egypt is punishable with up to 25 years in prison and a fine of up to 10 million Egyptian pounds ($640,000 US dollars.) The Ministry of Antiquities vets all applications from professional archaeologists who wish to participate in excavations. They protect their past.

But when you think of Egypt, you think of the Great Pyramids and the wonders of the tombs. So many of the pharaohs resting places have been plundered. Amateur archaeologists have done so much damage to irreplaceable artifacts that it is good to know Egyptian experts are using modern technologies to make accurate recordings, preserving the past in ways unavailable until recently.

However, the study of archeology is fascinating, and several avenues are open to you. For example, you can read, study images, and watch videos in your own home.

You could also visit your local museum. They often have interesting objects on view or may be hidden away behind the scenes so ask.

But you might want to get your hands dirty and participate in an actual excavation. Many digs do welcome amateurs. You can check out suggestions here: http://www.ubarchaeologist.com, but you need to contact the team involved directly.

So, if you have ever wanted to reach back in time to physically hold something that was last touched by someone many, many years ago, in that case, Egypt might stimulate your passion, but you will have to experience the thrill of finding ancient objects elsewhere.

PAPYRUS PAPERMAKING

The Ancient Egyptians were the first people to make a paper-like material from the papyrus plant, and our English word paper is derived from this. True paper-making took place in China during the Han dynasty (25–220 CE.) But the first paper-like writing sheet was papyrus from Egypt, about 3,000 years ago.

So, what is the difference between papyrus and paper?

The Egyptians made papyrus 'paper' from natural plants. The fibers are pressed and pounded together and dried. On the other hand, paper is made from fibers that have been macerated and disintegrated.

The papyrus water plant grew in the marshy delta of the river Nile, and there was plenty of it. The outer rind is first removed to make papyrus, and thin strips are sliced off the sticky fibrous inner pith lengthwise. The strips are laid side by side, and then a second layer of papyrus strips is applied on top at right angles. Finally, the double layer is pounded together to make one strong sheet. Sometimes glue was also used.

The final sheets were polished to make the surface smoother for writing. The Egyptians used papyrus to make sails, cords, mats, and cloth. Later the Greeks and then the Romans adopted papyrus as writing material.

You can make your own 'papyrus' at home and get an authentic-looking ancient effect. If you then decorate it with Egyptian hieroglyphics, you could make some exciting and unusual items; perhaps they could be used as cards or gifts.

This is how to make your own papyrus:

1. Cover your work surfaces – it can get messy. Lay out a paper towel.
2. Have glue ready – it might be wallpaper glue that needs mixing. Strong glue is not needed.
3. Place the glue in a flattish bowl.
4. Tear a brown paper bag into strips.
5. One by one, dip the strips of paper into the glue mix and place them side by side with the edges overlapping on the paper towel.
6. Smooth the surface out.
7. Do a second layer at right angles to the first and smooth out.
8. Let it dry.

9. Your paper is ready.

HIEROGLYPHICS

Hieroglyphics are attractive to look at, and for many years they were full of mystery. Egyptian tombs are full of them.

The word is Greek, although the writing is Egyptian. The name comes from 'Hiero,' which means 'holy,' and 'glyphics,' which means 'marks.' To ancient Egyptians, there was power in a name. That is why the pharaohs had their names inscribed in their tombs. It helped them to survive in the afterlife.

A breakthrough in deciphering these strange symbols came when Napoleon's troops discovered the Rosetta stone in 1799 when they invaded Egypt. This stone has hieroglyphs and a Greek translation, although it took about 20 years to decipher completely.

You read the hieroglyphs from left to right or from right to left. The figures always point to the start of the line so you can tell which direction to read it. And you start at the top. The pictures often represent what they show, but usually, the picture stands for a sound. Sometimes the same symbol can have two meanings. For example, a mouth image can mean a mouth or the sound 'r.'

While you can often guess the meaning, the symbolism is complex and can be confusing. But it is possible to work out how to 'spell' your name.

Why not make some 'papyrus' and decorate it with hieroglyphs? Spelling out your friend's name could make a unique and thoughtful birthday card, and learning about the hieroglyphs must surely challenge the brain.

COPTIC BOOK-BINDING

The early Christians in Egypt employed a type of book-binding called Coptic binding. This form of book-binding uses a thread to sew the layers together. A similar modern style of book-binding retains the name. But it took many years to change from storing writing in scrolls to storing it in books.

Originally the parchments were folded in half, and the sewing was done through the folded area. This made the edges uneven since the inner folded pages protruded and needed to be trimmed when the binding was done. When the book was first written, one had to determine how many pages were needed and how wide to make the margins.

Once single pages without folds were used, life became easier for the bookbinders.

The covers were usually sewn in and were often made from limp leather stiffened with papyrus, or something wooden.

Coptic binding is easy, and you can produce your own books this way. It works well for a series of sketches or a journal, and you don't need to have many pages. The internet has some good instructional videos, but it is just a matter of sewing one of the sides of the pages together with a continuous thread.

SENET

The game of senet was played as long ago as 5,000 years by the Egyptians. So popular was this game that it had been found among the funeral offerings in the graves of the dead, from pharaohs to the elite to commoners. Something to occupy them in the afterlife.

The boards could be highly decorated or simple grids – even drawings. The game is for two people; the board is marked on 30 squares in three rows of ten. Each player had between five and ten marked sticks, which they threw in turn. The aim was to progress along with the board, evading blocking movements by their opponent and getting rid of their pieces.

On the walls of the tombs of the New Kingdom, the game had taken on a religious significance, representing the path of the dead through the underworld. These boards have unique marks on the last five squares to show the arrival of eternity.

The boards were usually made from Egyptian faience, a common material used to make many small objects and ornaments. Some senet boards were made from wood. And if you are wondering what Egyptian faience is, here is a description taken from Wikipedia:

"Egyptian faience is a non-clay based ceramic composed of crushed quartz or sand, with small amounts of calcite lime and a mixture of alkalis, displaying surface vitrification due to the soda-lime-silica glaze often containing copper pigments to create a bright blue-green luster."

Since senet was so popular, it might be worth buying a board and having a few games. You could even buy several boards and start a senet playing club in your living room. Then, you might find out just why it was so popular.

SUMMARY

Egyptians have some unique interests that we can try our hand at, and the archeology of Egypt is the basis for many of these unique hobbies. Although amateur archaeologists are not welcome in Egypt, the subject can be an inspiration for hobbies such as papyrus paper making, Coptic book-binding, and learning about and writing hieroglyphics and the ancient game of senet.

Amateur Archeology
Papyrus Papermaking
Hieroglyphics – study and draw
Coptic Book-Binding
Senet

ZIMBABWE

Zimbabwe is a land of natural wonders. Victoria Falls is one of the seven natural wonders of the world, known as 'the smoke that thunders' in local languages. There are national parks full of wildlife, and the people have used the natural resources to produce some lovely craftwork. Music, dance, and song are a way of life.

They were building impressive cities of stone around 1,200 AD, including two great cities – Great Zimbabwe and Khami – and their walls survive to this day. There is a diverse population, and each ethnic group has its legends and myths and an oral recording of its stories, heroes, and past. In the daily life of Zimbabwe, the people combine the African and Western worlds. Ancestor worship continues, but about 75% also worship as Christians or Islam.

Traditional crafts and music continue to this day. Songs and stories are passed on in the rich culture of Zimbabwe.

I've chosen four hobbies you could pursue in your own way.

MBIRA INSTRUMENTAL MUSIC

The Shona people of Zimbabwe have a group of traditional musical instruments called the mbira. The basic design is a wooden board with metal tines attached. The instrument is held in the hands, and the tines are plucked with thumbs and forefingers.

For thousands of years, similar musical instruments have been played in Africa. The tines were originally made from bamboo and played over 3,000 years ago. Metal tines came later, around 1,500 years ago, and became popular among the Shona people, who called them 'mbira.'

There are many forms of mbira, but 'the voice of the ancestors' is heard in the mbira dzavadzimu and plays an integral part in religious ceremonies, weddings, and social meetings. In addition, traditional music is on the UNESCO Representative List of the Intangible Cultural Heritage of Humanity.

The mbira gave rise to the kalimba, a modern, popularized version exported from Africa in the late 1950s. It might be played by bands with electric guitars, drums, and horns and incorporate many songs taken from the Shona.

The sound can be unfamiliar to western ears. There are thousands of different tunings; adjacent tines vibrate, causing secondary harmonies, and shells and bottle tops might be added to the wooden board to increase the vibratory tone. This buzzing is said to attract the spirits of the dead. The layout of the tines can be idiosyncratic, with odd notes appearing when least expected. Intervals between notes differ from Western scales.

Just as the sounds are complex, so is the rhythm. Often a 3:2 cross-rhythm, the left hand playing bass and the right hand the melody.

It is possible to buy a mbira instrument, and there are videos on the internet to teach you how to play it. It would be not only exciting and entertaining but probably extremely difficult for one brought up only on western music to acquire competence on the mbira, but what a journey.

BEADWORK

Beads have been ornamental since ancient times and in most cultures. They have been used as money for trade, to adorn the person and clothes, and to make works of art. Initially, local items such as shells, wood, and even teeth were threaded and used as status symbols and decorations.

When glass beads were manufactured in bulk, they became essential items of trade. And now we are fortunate to have a huge variety of beads with all kinds of uses. Glass beads were imported to Zimbabwe in the 7th century from places as far away as Sri Lanka and the Persian Gulf. The Portuguese brought glass beads into the country to exchange for gold dust, ivory, and tobacco.

The beadwork of the BaTonga, of Zimbabwe and Zambia, is outstanding for the variety, color, and intricacy of the designs. Zimbabwe is known for bead wall art, tree decorations, and small animal ornaments. The most commonly chosen animals are their native wild animals, making them rather unique.

They also use glass beads to define the different stages of a woman's life, perhaps as a skirt for small girls with white beads that reflect the light and seem to express the joy of childhood. Traditional healers may wear distinctive beadwork to help identify their calling. The beads may work as charms against evil spirits or bring good luck to the wearer.

The little wire and bead animals look very cute, and there are kits available, so you could build up a collection of these ornaments or make some scintillating tree decorations.

BASKETRY

Crafts are an important source of income for many families in Zimbabwe, and the beautiful baskets produced are one of the most successful traditional crafts.

This is particularly true for the Tonga women in northwest Zimbabwe. They use materials found locally, such as grass, fronds from palm trees, and reeds. 'Binga' baskets, named for the town, use a hard vine and ilala palm.

Originally, these baskets were used for winnowing grain and are still used for this purpose. However, they are used for fruit, bread, placemats, dishes, or decorating walls. The patterns can be pretty intricate and decorated with natural tree-bark dyes. A simple over-and-under-weaving technique is employed, but a 16-inch diameter basket can take up to three days to finish. Finally, the coiled rim is completed using a herringbone pattern.

The designs are inspired by nature and learned through apprenticeship within families.

The export of these baskets is a welcome source of income for village families. Indeed, it has enabled many families to send their children to school.

Basketry is available to all of us. We may not be able to source local plants, but there are many alternatives, and many educational facilities hold basket weaving courses.

They are a practical and decorative addition to anyone's home.

MUBOORA UNE DOVI TRADITIONAL DISH

Muboora Une Dovi is a traditional African dish that comes from Zimbabwe. To create this delicious dish, combine pumpkin leaves, tomato, onion, salt, baking soda, peanut butter, and oil. Carefully wash your pumpkin leaves, then simmer in a pot of boiling water with salt and baking soda until fully cooked.

Ingredients (serves 3 - 4)

1 bundle muboora (young pumpkin leaves and stems)
2 cups water
1 tsp baking soda
1 tsp salt
1 Tbsp oil
1 tomato, roughly chopped
2 Tbsp smooth peanut butter
1 onion, roughly chopped

Method

- Once cooked, drain the excess water and set aside while you make the sauce.
- Heat oil in a saucepan over medium heat. Add onion and cook until softened.
- Add tomato, stir well and cover with a lid. Cook for 5 minutes, then stir in peanut butter.

- Mix well, adding enough boiling water to make a thick paste.
- Add your pumpkin leaves and combine.

Muboora is typically served with sadza (Zimbabwe staple) or rice. Why not start a monthly supper club in your community as a hobby? Each month could be a different country to focus on. What a fantastic way to learn about other cultures while enjoying delicious food.

SHONA SCULPTURES

Hanc sculpture is a relatively modern term, but the Shona people have been working with stone for hundreds of years. For example, the Great Zimbabwe Settlement was an 11th - 15th-century town built of stone and housing up to 1,800 people. This is now a world heritage site for the Shona people.

But now, the Shona sculpture means artistic stone-carved works. The name Shona comes from the mix of tribes known as Shona. The sculptures have close links with cultural and spiritual practices many still practiced today. Only relatively recently has this Zimbabwe's art achieved worldwide recognition, which is still evolving.

Millions of years ago, an extremely rich vein of Serpentine rock, stretching for hundreds of miles, was laid down and is now on the surface. Many of the stones used are members of the Serpentine family, and they have a range of colors from dark green-black to brighter but less common colors. While Springstone is the most commonly used stone, many different varieties of stone are carved to produce a range of styles and colors.

Opal Stone is another softer variant than serpentine, smooth and glossy, with specks of red and blue. With its purple or green coloring and lighter markings, Cobalt stones are brittle and apt to break, but the results can look marvelous.

Dolomite is soft and suitable for more significant works, and sometimes it is tinged with iron or has transparent white crystals, giving the finished product a pearl-like appearance.

Butter Jade might look like butter, but it is hard and long-lasting. Despite its name, it is not a true jade and is rare outside South Africa. Sapolite, lemon opal, and leopard stone are other variants the sculpture might use.

Carving stone might not be a suitable hobby for you, but collecting them could be. They would certainly make an unusual collection and could lead to social contacts in many countries.

SUMMARY

Zimbabwe is a country where people have embraced music and song to tell their history. The traditional Mbira musical instrument might take a great deal of practice to perfect playing, but listening to the different intonations can stimulate the brain. Their crafts reflect the incredible wildlife found in their natural parks, and the cute little wire and bead animals plus the wall art are things that would be possible to enjoy at home. Basketry is a hobby that can be DIY at home or as a social gathering, and collecting the Shona people of Zimbabwe's stone sculptures is a hobby growing worldwide.

Mbira instrumental music
Beadwork
Basketry
Muboora Une Dovi Traditional Dish
Shona sculptures

MEXICO

Mexico is full of color and movement, and humor. From their masks to their dances, from their art to their care for children. The people of Mexico have a rich and entertaining set of crafts and hobbies.

Like most of us, they go shopping, read and watch television. Family life is important, and children take an active part in the social life of Mexicans. So, large family meals, caravans, and camping are popular activities, and with the sunny beaches and blue sea, they have a wide choice of places to go.

I have chosen six activities you might enjoy, so let's dive in.

JARABE TAPATÍO DANCE

The Jarabe Tapatío is the national dance of Mexico. It is often known as the Mexican Hat dance in the USA, but it is far more than that and has a somewhat checkered history.

The theme of the dance is the courtship of a man with a lady he meets at a party. The dance starts by dancing around a sombrero, hence the alternative name. At first, she rejects his advances, but ultimately, she accepts them, and he may raise his hat to hide a kiss.

This dance originated in Western Mexico during the 19th century, although some elements predate this, going back to the Spanish Zambra. The music, composed by Jesus Gonzalez Rubio, and the dance represent Mexico.

Why Jarabe? This is derived from the Arabic for "mixed herbs" and reflects the mix of different Mexican dances and music. While other versions of Jarabe exist, the Tapatio version is the best known.

Originally, the Jarabe Tapatio was danced only by women to avoid religious censorship. By 1790 mixed couples performed, but soon after, the dance was banned as Spanish colonial and religious authorities thought it morally offensive. The result was that the dance became even more popular, and people held dances illegally as a form of protest.

After independence in 1861, the dance became even more popular, widely celebrated in festivals and fiestas. The dance is still taught in most Mexican schools to this day.

To learn how to do the Jarabe Tapatio, you either need to study videos, and there are several on the internet or attend classes. Dancing the Jarabe Tapatio would be enormous fun, and watching a performance would make for great entertainment.

MEXICAN YARN ART

Mexico is well known for the bright colors and artistic talent of the people. Yarn art is no exception.

Traditional Neirikas are yarn paintings that the people of Huichol make. They make their own glue from beeswax and tree resin, then paste it onto a board. First, a pattern is scratched on the surface of the wax. Then the yarn is pressed into it to make a bold, colorful pattern, filling in all the spaces; it is left to harden. The designs themselves represent local myths and tales and illustrate everyday life.

The Huichol people of Mexico live in small villages in the Sierra Madre. The gods are essential; there will be houses for the gods or even caves, and people bring gifts, such as flowers, feathers, prayer bowls, and yarn art. They hope their gifts will bring them luck.

What the gift symbolizes matters. Neirika means 'face,' and the face depicted might be the face of the wind or the face of the harvest. They might be expressing a wish; a face of water or a serpent might mean a longing for rain, and the face of the sun a wish for a good harvest.

Maybe you have a wish you could make a face for? Or maybe you just enjoy making something attractive and unusual.

You can also try making your own yarn art. You will need a stiff card for the base, white glue (PVA works well), scissors, and several colored yarns. You may find a toothpick useful for scratching your pattern, and you will probably need plenty of paper towels.

There are many uses for these yarn pictures. You can use them to decorate boxes, cover notebooks, and create cards and pictures for your wall, and they make perfect gifts.

The internet has many inspiring examples, but you may prefer to think up your own patterns to represent a much-loved pet or a swirly sea scene with colorful fish. The possibilities are endless.

WORRY DOLLS

Worry dolls originated in Guatemala but are widely popular in Mexico, and for good reason.

They are small, hand-made little dolls that one can use in several ways to relieve anxiety and worry. This is especially helpful for children.

The legend goes that a Sun god gave a Mayan princess called Ixmucane a special gift. This gift would let her resolve any problem that might worry her. The traditional way to use a worry doll was to tell the doll about your worries and then place the doll under your pillow and go to sleep. In the morning, you would wake up with all the skills and wisdom needed to solve the problem.

Modern psychology shows that, indeed, our brains do sort things out during our sleep. It's important to realize that this process does not teach us that there are no worries, but it is a tool for helping us deal with what life throws at us.

These little dolls are often homemade, from wool, wire, pressed paper, and little pieces of colorful textiles. While most dolls are tiny, under 3 inches tall, they can be made to any size to suit you. Traditionally, they are dressed in a Mayan style of clothing.

Anyone can make their own worry dolls from familiar everyday things like popsicle sticks, cloth from old clothes, sellotape, or glue. Or maybe collect stuff from a nature walk like sticks, feathers, etc. It can be a bit more exciting if you have some googly eyes for them. Making your own dolls makes it unique for you.

MEXICAN MASKS

For thousands of years, the people of Mexico have been making masks. They played their part in rituals, theater, and processions. Religious ceremonies and burials are where the wealthiest dead had masks made from precious materials such as jade and decorated with shells.

When the Spanish arrived, they adapted the masks to the Catholic faith.

The masks are still a part of the culture, especially in 'Lucha Libre,' which is a form of wrestling. The use of an animal mask was said to give the strength and cunning of the animal to the fighter. Some of these masks are handed down from father to son for several generations. But in some matches, the loser must remove his mask, which may never be worn again.

Many other popular mask themes include animals, demons, and fantasy figures. Dancing and many other uses for the masks are still around. Religions and fiestas amalgamated, and many masked dancers participated in festivals and Holy Week. Halloween is a great excuse to create and wear a fabulous mask.

Although traditional masks are often made from wood, many other materials, including paper and card, papier mache, feathers, and leather, can also be used. They are often highly decorated and brilliantly colored. Even real teeth might be added, or maybe real horns from goats, deer, or cows.

Mask-making is something anyone can do. If you have grandchildren, they might like to try their hand at making masks. All you have to do is provide some materials and a little time. You might even decide to host a small party where wearing a mask is part of the fun, and there could be a competition for the most original mask on display.

SCRATCH ART

What is scratch art? You may know it as Art-foil, foil art, or even engraving art. And it is a little like engraving. Since you scratch off the black inky surface to reveal the color underneath, the results can be quite stunning.

Scratch art all started in England and France in the 19th century. Then, it was easy to reproduce as an alternative to metal wood or linoleum engraving, but now Mexico has developed a unique way of using it. The designs can be intricate, precise, and sometimes highly colored.

First, you scratch the top coat, usually black ink, but why not use different colors? The base may be white or multi-colored. Then, color can be painted on, and even that layer can be further scratched to make subtle changes to your pattern. Once complete, you will want to preserve your art by varnishing it, framing it, and hanging it.

Simple kits, for starters, are easy to find. When you get more skilled, you can paint in background colors, add glitter if you wish, and make unique pictures to adorn your walls.

TREE OF LIFE

The beautiful trees of life are pottery, artistic creations traditional to central Mexico. While pottery has been as long ago as 1800 BC, the tree of life has evolved over the centuries. The original clay figures were unpainted, but later color was added, and later still, the Christian religion influenced their design as a way to tell the stories of the bible. The Spanish priests destroyed images of the ancient gods, replacing them with Christian symbols.

The original Christian trees of life depicted the story of Adam and Eve and the Garden of Eden. Still, popular designs also included Noah, and the Ark. Modern trees of life can show many themes, including flowers, mermaids, the cosmos, Mexican dances, and animals.

A traditional Christian tree typically has an image of God at the top. Beneath him is the creation of the world in 7 days with the sun and moon, Adam and Eve, and the serpent. Finally, at the bottom, Adam is cast out of Eden.

The trees are made from clay and covered with small, brightly-colored, hand-painted images. The trees are usually between 26 and 60 cm tall, although there are some giant ones in public places. The clay is fired at low temperatures in gas ovens. A large one can take several years to complete, but the basic shape is somewhat like a candelabra, with arms to hold the tiny clay figures.

Every year there are competitions, including a 'Human Tree of Life.' In 2006, people from 63 ethnic groups dressed in native costumes and made a human pyramid. They had a message – peace in the world.

But how can you make this a hobby?

There are instructional videos on the internet for making them, but making the clay skeleton and figures in your kitchen would be hard. There are two alternatives:

You could buy one or collect a few and enjoy studying them. Read about them and decipher the stories behind them. Or you could make something similar from a card, paper, wire, glue, and paint. The old-fashioned pipe-cleaners make easy-to-make skeletons for small figurines. You could tell your own story and create your own Tree of Life, perhaps telling your own life story.

SUMMARY

As you can see, a great variety of hobbies are undertaken enthusiastically by the Mexican people. But color, brightness, and movement can be seen in all of them. The Jarabe dance tells a story. The masks illustrate stories, and the worry dolls create an excellent listening ear. So let your imagination go wild with the yarn or scratch art, and put everything together with a tree of life.

Jarabe Tapatio Dance
Yarn Art
Worry dolls
Masks
Scratch Art
Tree of life

PHILIPPINES

Why is the Philippines spelled with "ph," yet the people know themselves as Filipinos?

The name is derived from King Phillip the second of Spain, who reigned in the 16th Century. Spain was a seafaring nation whose sailors explored this area and instituted the Roman Catholic religion, which remains predominant today.

The Philippines consists of 7,641 islands. Over 5,000 islands still have no names on international maps, yet the Philippines make up the biggest archipelago in the world.

Filipinos know how to live a good life with family and friends, and music and singing are important elements of their way of life. The internet, skillfully used, plays a huge part as well. Many of their pastimes are social, from games such as basketball to wandering about the shopping malls.

So let us look more at some of the hobbies Filipinos enjoy.

KARAOKE

Singing is a national pastime; everyone loves to sing, whether they can or not!

Every opportunity to sing is enthusiastically taken. House parties, visitors to the home, and celebrations of all kinds are an excuse to sing; no reason is needed to burst into song. Children are surrounded by the sound of singing as they grow up and carry on singing as adults.

Karaoke has become a part of everyday life. Most Filipinos have a karaoke machine or a 'magic sing' microphone. This device makes your television a karaoke machine, easy to bring out when visitors arrive or parties are being hosted.

Legend says that karaoke began in Kobe in Japan. A certain band failed to turn up, so the bar owner was inspired to invite customers to take their place on the stage instead. The first karaoke machine was invented in Kobe when an orchestra went on strike, so the management substituted a machine.

You can find karaoke arcades along the streets in the Philippines, and these are popular places to visit in the evenings for a good sing-along. And no one minds if you are out of tune, it's the enthusiasm that counts.

Karaoke is a social activity, and once tried, it is fun for adults and children, and you can buy magic-sing equipment on the internet very easily. So, why not have a go? Invite a few friends around and have a ball.

PICNICS IN THE PARK

Eating out is about bonding with family and friends, and Filipinos always eat out.

With their warm weather and scenic parks, picnics are a natural way to spend time. And in the Philippines, there is one great advantage common to many Asiatic countries; one can find ready-prepared food in street stalls. So, it is easy to buy the food and take it to the nearest park to eat it. Moreover, the bought food is often cheaper than do-it-yourself cooking, as well as convenient.

However, when you make a barbeque, everyone has their share of the preparation, and everyone must wait for the meal to be ready. Nevertheless, it's an excellent way for family bonding, and Filipinos make the most of it. Indeed, cooking for Filipinos is about spending time with your family and doing something enjoyable together. And who doesn't enjoy good food and the outdoors?

In the Philippines, there is a particular word for just strolling outdoors – Lamyerda. Maybe with friends, perhaps time out for yourself, or simply an excuse to sample the delicious local ice-cream sorbets.

Have you tried taking a barbeque to your local park with your friends or family? Setting it up and cooking your favorite barbeque food? Some parks do not allow this, but most places permit it as long as you clear up afterward. A barbeque is a pleasant way to meet up with people you may not know very well or with your closest friends and family.

MALLING

What is 'malling?'

Malling means hanging out in the shopping mall. Malling is a serious business in the Philippines. There are about 865 malls, and each acts as a 'mini-economy.' Some of these malls are gigantic.

The malls are air-conditioned, which makes a pleasant break from what might be a hot and humid day. Filipinos go to the malls to cool down and meet their friends who are also escaping the heat.

And there is plenty to interest you. Window shopping, checking out the latest fashions, buying presents, or even just a pleasant walk. And if you get a bit peckish, you can find stalls selling local dishes or restaurants to rest your aching feet. Be warned; if you visit the Philippines, you may need to buy an extra suitcase.

Some of the special Filipino items for sale or display include pearls, silk, and baskets. Bamboo articles are popular, and specialist Barako coffee beans are worth sampling.

Have you explored your local mall? Maybe you have to drive a little distance to find one? Have you chatted to any of the vendors and sampled their wares? Have you ever eaten at the mall or met friends for coffee or lunch? Or have you ever simply been there wandering about amidst the bustle without any clear aim in mind? If the weather is poor, malling is a great way to get exercise and stay dry.

BASKETBALL

Basketball – is the most popular sport in the Philippines.

Taught at school, played after school in the alleyways and street corners, and encouraged in the gyms, basketball is followed by almost everyone in the Philippines. Everyone knows the rules, and most Filipinos are avid followers of the sport. In fact, according to Nike, they sell more of their sportswear to the Philippines than anywhere else except the USA and China.

A sport requiring little equipment makes this game accessible to everyone, young and old, rich and poor. You can sit at home or join a group in a club or bar and watch it, or, if you are active, you can join a team and participate. Maybe you have family members who are on a team you can support?

So important is basketball to Filipinos that elections might be postponed if they clash with the National Basketball Association (NBA) Finals. And, of course, you can follow the game live on television. A fast-action, fun-filled sport, it's easy to get involved and cheer for your team.

You could get interested in watching basketball on television if there is no team playing near you.

SOCIAL MEDIA

The Philippines is known as the 'text capital of the world' because of the massive number of text messages sent.

The figures are staggering. Filipinos use social media more than any other people worldwide, and the average user spends 11 hours a day on the internet. That's 60% more than the global average. Filipinos spend over four hours a day using social media.

Friendships are essential to Filipinos, so it's no surprise that Facebook is the most popular medium, with 99% of adults having Facebook accounts. But for influencers, Instagram and YouTube lead the way, with Facebook and Twitter also popular. Filipinos know that the people you know are the most valuable tool for getting on in life.

The Filipino people are avid readers and write blogs and upload photos and videos. In fact, this is where people know how to get the most out of the media, to understand the enormous benefits and the ways it can enhance your life.

Do you understand computers and smartphones? Are you taking advantage of the many benefits available? And importantly, are you also protecting your online presence?

SUMMARY

Laughter and singing, socializing in person and over the internet, and family and friends make for an energetic yet balanced way of life. Karaoke is everywhere, and picnics and barbeques in the park are popular. Basketball and malling are two somewhat different ways to have fun, and social media is a way of life in the Philippines.

Karaoke
Picnics in the Park
Malling
Basketball
Social media

THE UNIVERSAL HOBBY

Our final hobby is a challenge!

It has been gratifying exploring various countries and plucking out activities older people do in their spare time.

Almost everywhere, people play football, watch television and read. Some countries have hobbies that are so unique to the country that they cannot be exported, such as cheetah walking and wadi trails.

Here is your challenge. Can you find more countries with unique hobbies that one could do or modify to enjoy at home? Of course, they must be suitable for older people, not too expensive and must not entail visiting that country.

There are about 195 countries worldwide, so there is plenty to choose from. If you are interested in populations, you can watch the changes as they happen at: https://www.worldometers.info/.

I hope you have enjoyed your journey through 21 countries and that you feel inspired to try out a new hobby or two.

FINAL THOUGHTS

This has been another whirlwind adventure around the globe; discovering, learning, and pondering new hobbies to try at home. Hobbies worldwide are varied and often show a fascinating insight into the history of that country and the people living there.

Even if you cannot replicate the exact hobby, hopefully, it has given you ideas for engaging activities and crafts to inspire your next project. While some of these hobbies might appear less unique, they may be a reminder of an activity you once loved that you could participate in again? So, how might you adjust or refresh this hobby to suit you at this present time?

For many, touring the world is not an option due to the high cost of travel, or maybe your mobility is not what it once was. On the other hand, for some, reading about all these far away places might have you planning your next trip. Either way, I hope that the pages of this book have energized you, even if in some small way.

As discussed in the last chapter, perhaps you are now curious to research more hobbies from around the world? With about 195 countries globally, there is still a lot of territory to cover.

With your new finds, feel free to write to me and let me know what you've discovered so I can consider that hobby in a future book. You may reach me at:

ravina@ravinachandra.com, and I look forward to hearing from you.

FROM THE AUTHOR

Thank you so much for reading 101 *More* Ways to Enjoy Retirement. Please don't forget to write a brief review at the retailer where you purchased this book. I am grateful for all feedback, and your review will help other readers decide whether to read this book too. Follow this link to leave a review:

Interested in staying in touch to hear about any of my future books or projects?

Contact me at ravina@ravinachandra.com
or visit www.ravinachandra.com

INDEX

IMAGE CREDITS

Chile
UFO over Trees by ursatii from Getty Images, under the Canva Pro Content License.

Croatia
Christmas Markets by clubfoto from Getty Images Signature, under the Canva Pro Content License.

Egypt
Ancient Egyptian Hieroglyphics by wwing from Getty Images Signature, under the Canva Pro Content License. Papyrus Artisan at work by siculodoc from Getty Images, under the Canva Pro Content License.

Estonia
Tallinn by RudyBalasko from Getty Images, under the Canva Pro Content License.

Iceland
Icelandic Horses by stannic from Getty Images, under the Canva Pro Content License.

India
Herbs and spices by Studio Doros from Getty Images, under the Canva Pro Content License.
Ireland (Éire)
Belgium Tervuren Herding Ducks by MereW322 Getty Images, under the Canva Pro Content License.
Jamaica
Spicy Grilled Jerk Chicken on a plate by from_my_-point_of_view from Getty Images, under the Canva Pro Content License.
Liechtenstein
Stamp Collection by Blade_kostas from Getty Images Signature, under the Canva Pro Content License.
Mexico
Worry Dolls by elanneivy from Getty Images Pro, under the Canva Pro Content License.
Traditional Handmade Mayan, Mexican Mask by Maciejen Grabowicz from Getty Images, under the Canva Pro Content License.
Mongolia
Yurt in Mongolia by pascalou95 from Getty Images, under the Canva Pro Content License.
Nepal
Felt Flowers by agalma from Getty Images, under the Canva Pro Content License.
Oman
Spice Souk by cengizkarbakus from Getty Images, under the Canva Pro Content License.

Philippines

Smiling Sporty Filipina Female Basketball Player with Basketball by dtiberio from Getty Images, under the Canva Pro Content License.

Samoa

Wedding Cake Decoration by W Jayasinghe from Getty Images, under the Canva Pro Content License.

Scotland

Traditional Scottish Highland Dancing by Lucassek from Getty Images, under the Canva Pro Content License.

South Africa

Malva Pudding and custard by CarlaMc from Getty Images Signature, under the Canva Pro Content License.

South Korea

Sunrise at Jeju Do Seongsan Ilchulbong, Jeju Island by Noppasim Wongchum from Getty Images, under the Canva Pro Content License.

Sweden

Untitled by StockSnap from Pixabay, under the Canva Pro Content License.

Turkey

Stray cats in Turkey city by ValeriMak from Getty Images, under the Canva Pro Content License.

Zimbabwe

African men designing and producing beadwork by THEGIFT777 from Getty Images Signature, under the Canva Pro Content License.